PRAISE FOR *THE ART OF STRATEGIC*

"Understanding and putting into play strategic communication is a key component of police leadership. The concepts throughout this book provide a solid framework upon which the profession can build the legitimacy and trust needed to be successful in any community. As a testament to his life's work, the tools and tactics contained within these pages will help departments navigate contemporary communication challenges and opportunities."

—Judy Pal, CEO 10-8 Communications LLC,
Author *Strategic Communication for Law Enforcement Executives,*
former Assistant Commissioner New York City Police Department,
Chief of Staff Milwaukee and Baltimore Police, and communications
lead Atlanta, Savannah, and Halifax Regional Police (Canada)

"At no time in history in law enforcement is it more important than ever to master the craft of communicating when it matters. Chief Cook builds upon his decades of experience to present an easy-to-read blueprint on how to bolster trust, manage critical incidents, and navigate controversies."

—Alex Del Carmen, Author of *Racial Profiling Policing: Beyond*
***the Basics,* Professor and Associate Dean of the College of Liberal**
and Fine Arts and the School of Criminology, Criminal Justice,
and Strategic Studies at Tarleton State University

"*The Art of Strategic Communication* is a masterpiece work in the field of public relations and community outreach. Filled with insightful strategies, communities will be better served through proactive approaches to connect with residents, businesses, and visitors. Chris most certainly has made strategic communication an art form."

—Anne E. Schwartz, author of *Monster: The True*
Story of the Jeffrey Dahmer Murders

"Chief Cook is a legend in crisis communications, powerful media relations, and the strategic use of social media. As one of the best in the profession, *The Art of Strategic Communication* provides invaluable insights to get leaders and communicators up and running with immediate action items. This is a must-read book for practitioners and those who supervise them about how to get your message out in a timely and accurate manner and in ways that the message will be easily absorbed."

—Julie Parker, President & CEO Julie Parker Communications, Former Director of Media Relations Prince George's County (MD) and Fairfax County (VA) Police Departments, Former ABC7 News Reporter

"The ability of any police department to effectively serve the community relies almost exclusively on police officials effectively communicating and building public trust across various stakeholders with differing life experiences and perspectives. Chief Cook excels in meeting peoples' communication needs, and his real-world experience and proven track record make him one of the most insightful leaders in strategic communication across the country."

—Will D. Johnson, Chief Special Agent BNSF Railway Police, Police Chief of Arlington, Texas (Ret.)

"Absolutely a phenomenal guidebook on applying strategy to your communication efforts. Christopher hit on the topic areas that matter most to police leaders and strategic communication advisors."

—Kristen Ziman, bestselling Author of *Reimagining Blue: Thoughts on Life, Leadership, and a New Way Forward in Policing,* Police Chief Aurora IL (Ret.)

THE ART OF STRATEGIC COMMUNICATION

THE
ART
OF
STRATEGIC
COMMUNICATION

A POLICE CHIEF'S GUIDE TO MASTERING SOUNDBITES, STORYTELLING, AND COMMUNITY ENGAGEMENT

CHRISTOPHER COOK

INDIE BOOKS
INTERNATIONAL

The Art of Strategic Communication™ is a pending trademark of Christopher Cook. www.policepio.com, www.sheriffpio.com, www.strategypio.com, www.strategicadvisorbook.com, and www. policechiefcook.com are all intellectual properties of First Responder Media Consultants, LLC registered with the Texas Secretary of State.

Facebook®, Instagram® are registered trademarks of Meta Platforms, Inc.
YouTube®, Android®, Google Alerts®, Google Podcasts® are registered trademarks of Google, LLC.
TikTok® is a registered trademark of TikTok, Ltd.
Snapchat® is a registered trademark of Snap, Inc.
Vimeo® is a registered trademark of Vimeo.com, Inc.
Hootsuite® is a registered trademark of Hootsuite Media, Inc.
IOS® is a registered trademark of Cisco
Canva® is a registered trademark of Canva Party, LTD.
Lucidpress® and Marq® are registered trademarks of Lucid Software, Inc.
Affinity Publisher®, Affinity Photo®, and Affinity Designer® are registered trademarks of Serif Europe, Ltd.
Adobe InDesign®, Adobe Photoshop®, Adobe Illustrator®, Adobe Lightroom CC®, Lightroom Mobile®, Adobe Stock®, and Adobe Premier® are registered trademarks of Adobe, Inc.
Phonto® is a registered trademark of Polymath Company, Ltd.
Magic Eraser® is a registered trademark of The Proctor and Gamble Company
PicCollage® is a registered trademark of Cardinal Blue Software, Inc.
Motion VFX® and Motion Array® are registered trademarks of Artist Ltd. Corporation, Israel
Envato® and AudioJungle® are registered trademarks of Envato Pty. Ltd. LLC, Australia
Fiverr® is a registered trademark of Fiverr International Ltd. Corporation, Israel
Shutterstock® is a registered trademark of Shutterstock, Inc. Corporation
iStockPhoto® is a registered trademark of iStockphoto LP Limited Partnership, Canada
Blur Photo Background® is a registered trademark of NCH Software Corporation
xPro® is a registered trademark of Astral IP Enterprise LLC, Canada
Mentionlytics® is a registered trademark of Mentionalytics LTD. United Kingdom
Boardreader® is a registered trademark of Effyis, Inc.
DJI® is a registered trademark of SZ DJI Technology Co., Ltd, LLC, China
RØDE® is a registered trademark of Freedman Electronics, Pty., LTD.
Critical Mention® is a registered trademark of Critical Mention, Inc.
Lume Cube® is a registered trademark of Lume Cube, Inc.
Motion VFX® and Motion Array® are registered trademarks of Artist, Ltd., Israel
Apple®, iPod®, Apple Podcasts®, iWatermark®, Final Cut Pro X®, and Mac® are registered trademarks of Apple, Inc.
Avid® is a registered trademark of Avid Technology, Inc.
Vegas Pro® is a registered trademark of Magix Software Fed. Rep. Germany.
Windows® is a registered trademark of Microsoft Corporation
Axon Investigate® is a registered trademark of Axon Enterprise, Inc.
Storyblocks® is a registered trademark of Footage Firm, Inc.
Spotify® is a registered trademark of Spotify AB
Soundstripe® is a registered trademark of Soundstripe, Inc
Buzzfeed® is a registered trademark of Buzzfeed, Inc.
iHeart® is a registered trademark of iHeart, LLC
The National Certified Public Manager accredits Certified Public Manager®

ISBN-13: 978-1-957651-70-5
Library of Congress Control Number: 2024905129
Designed by theBookDesigners
INDIE BOOKS INTERNATIONAL®, INC.
2511 WOODLANDS WAY
OCEANSIDE, CA 92054
www.indiebooksintl.com

This book is dedicated to the guardians of society—
law enforcement officers, who represent the thin blue line—
and the strategic communication advisors and leaders who tell
their heroic and brave stories.

The nobility of policing requires the noblest of character.
Dr. Stephen R. Covey.[1]

CONTENTS

INTRODUCTION

While this book was written from a niche background, with stories and experiences drawn from the law enforcement profession, the principles can equally be applied to the entire spectrum representing public safety, emergency services, and government: fire, ambulance, medical, emergency management, local and state governments, education, military, and politics. The tools and strategies are universal.

Whether you're a policymaker or in the field, these concepts are presented for real-world application. They are written from the author's experience as a senior command-level executive, chief spokesperson, chief of staff, and ultimately chief of police—spanning almost three decades at agencies large (among the top fifty largest jurisdictions in the US) and small (less than fifty sworn officers).

Every police chief knows that you have a limited time in the chair. The clock starts the day you accept the appointment. The question is not how long but whether you do everything possible to make a positive difference in the organization and your community. Law enforcement executives are always one step away from wearing out their welcome.

The adage of the "buck stops here" has no truer meaning than with law enforcement executives. While the journey can certainly be rewarding, leading a police force, or being responsible for communications, the fact remains that you are occupying a temporary space. You're balancing community needs with resource and fiscal constraints. You must keep the workforce engaged while also building relationships with those your agency serves. You must balance time, calendar management, and energy. Oh, and by the way, don't neglect your family or overexert yourself to the detriment of your loved ones. It only takes one wrong move for all the pieces to fall around you. Bad decisions and the resulting mayhem are typically rooted in a lack of strategy and failure to communicate properly.

Think back to all the times you experienced an unfavorable working relationship. Did you ever think about how the relationship came off the rails? Often, you can trace the situation back to communication. Maybe the relationship got off to the wrong start. Maybe the other person felt slighted due to noncommunication. The point is we maintain productive and positive relationships through appropriate communication.

This is no different, no matter which organization. Having a strategy centers on having a master plan. In professional sports, there is a game plan. When building homes, there are blueprints. SWAT commanders have a set of tactics to approach incidents. Strategy for law enforcement organizations is all about planning and directing law enforcement operations and service delivery. From a comms perspective, strategy involves knowing your audience and developing tools and mediums to get the message out. That's why you were hired.

The most important tenet of strategy is communication. As executives, we transmit ideas. We must convey what the agency is doing. We present data and reports. We relay crime information. We divulge updates on major incidents. We disclose news as appropriate. We communicate across many different channels: in-person meetings, phone calls, briefings, media, videos, social media, and other forms. We communicate every single day.

As a profession, we need to be strategic about communication. We must determine our audience and adapt communication strategies to increase transparency, build trust, and encourage active community participation. If we get this right, our people are better trusted, and our communities are better served.

In today's fast-paced environment, the speed at which communication travels and the resounding calls for police accountability demonstrate a need for purposeful communications embedded in a strategic mindset. This is not hard. It does, however, require intentional and methodical thinking. It requires planning and goal setting. It also necessitates an ongoing review of strategies so that tweaks can be made to improve the agency, thereby strengthening the community.

Communication and strategy start with decision-making. Everything we do in policing comes with tradeoffs and risks. Do we release a video seeking the public's help on a case with the possibility of spreading fear, or do we allow detectives more time to work the case and risk the suspect reoffending? If faced with officer misconduct, should we hold a press conference or just disseminate a news release? Do we sit for interviews or simply release a statement on a force incident? Communication, or the lack thereof, requires constant assessment and decision-making.

The stakes are too high not to understand strategic communication. Technology abounds all around us. Social media rules the world. Video content is shared everywhere. People demand information and even share unvetted news across various platforms. Welcome to the new world of policing.

This book is a distillation of many lessons learned over the years. My goal is to assist your team with developing a sound and prudent strategy for communicating well.

Readers will also understand the almighty sound bite. A sound bite in journalism basically refers to a short phrase or sentence that captures the essence of what the speaker is trying to talk about. In the policing world, the sound bite is everything. Reporters, producers, and photojournalists know when someone hits a great sound bite. We can hope for a great sound bite, but we need to be intentional about developing a sound bite that resonates with your audience and conveys the main points of your conversation. Sound bites are not only required for news stories but can also be intertwined into visual and audio storytelling, as you will see.

This book is organized into three sections. The first part deals with the why. Everyone always wants to know the why. Why is strategic communication important? Why should your agency have a strategic communication advisor or public information officer, even if that duty falls to you? Once we understand the why, we will commit to excellence in strategic communication.

The next section is the how. We will discuss industry best practices on managing media, engaging on social media, handling critical incidents, and many other crucial aspects that deal with comms. This book leverages firsthand experience and expertise from some of the best in the business.

The final section brings the entire discussion together. Executives and communicators will learn to create a strategic communication plan and a crisis plan, assess situations and incidents, choose a path forward, execute plans, and evaluate the effectiveness of the communication strategy. This is where community engagement reaches its pinnacle—based upon strategic thinking, strategic execution, and strategic follow-up.

The bulk of my career and successes are directly tied to being able to communicate well. I have seen firsthand the litany of problems during communication failures across our profession. I know friends who have lost their jobs simply because they are unwilling to get in front of controversies. I have seen cases blow up based on a lack of strategy.

I have also seen the positive when communication is carried out expertly, with strategy as the guiding factor. This is why I wrote this book. I do not want you to experience some of the avoidable failures during my early tenure as a police executive. I sincerely hope you never have to experience a catastrophic incident in your jurisdiction. But know this: if a critical incident comes knocking on your door, you will have a resource guide to help you through it.

PART I

WHY STRATEGIC COMMUNICATION?

CHAPTER 1

WHY SHOULD LEADERS AND ADVISORS CARE ABOUT COMMUNICATION?

On March 3, 1991, a bystander took a video of Rodney King being beaten by four police officers in Los Angeles. This horrific incident was televised nationally, leading to significant rioting, loss of trust, and millions in damage. While many law enforcement agencies at the time hadn't been putting a lot of strategy into engaging with communities through the media, it was clear that a national conversation about policing and race was occurring in America. The video of a beating at the hands of law enforcement was placed front and center before our country. Perceptions about the role of the police played out across dinner tables in Main Street, USA.

Policing was different when I started. When I graduated from the police academy in the mid-1990s, there was no training in communication. Instructors didn't talk about the media. While the curriculum touched on history, the British father of modern policing, Sir Robert Peel, was only mentioned in passing, with little information provided about the complex origins of American policing as an institution. Compliance was achieved through brute force. People did what we told them to do. It was a different era, long before mobile phones with cameras became commonplace. Most academies focused on the physical side of maintaining command presence through conditioning and fitness. Verbal judo, de-escalation, procedural justice, and relational policing weren't in existence yet—at least to the level of importance that professional, modern, and noble departments hold as valuable in today's environment.

Dashcams were starting to find their way into agencies as the twentieth century ended, as an effort to thwart some of the challenges of the rise of handheld camcorders and video that were negatively affecting the profession. Even though there was no YouTube until 2005, citizens routinely filmed police interactions and shared them with news organizations. Two television names synonymous with the creation of COPS, John Langley and Malcolm Barbour, found success through reality television by riding with police officers and showcasing patrol shifts.

It was common to have newspaper journalists and television reporters assigned to crime beats. In some agencies, reporters had office space at the stations where they would collect daily crime blotters and prepare stories. Radio Shack had pioneered scanners that could listen to police radios over the airwaves. There was no encryption back then. When a major incident occurred, a news van wrapped in television station graphics would roll to a scene with a photographer and reporter.

The purpose of sharing this history is to demonstrate a fundamental shift in communication that could be traced to almost three decades ago. Many issues plaguing our profession in the early 1990s still harm us today. Police leaders could no longer hide behind their doors when stories emerged. Agencies were on the hook to message their communities. Communities wanted information. The media wanted agencies to be responsive.

We are at a crossroads. We can either let others define our profession, or we can tell our own story. Policing is made up of a patchwork of thousands of different agencies. My home state of Texas has almost three thousand police departments representing eighty thousand peace officers.[2] Across the US, more than eighteen thousand agencies exist. Most are small, some are midsized, and a few cover large urban centers. They may have local, county, state, or federal jurisdiction. My point is that narratives are being created in the name of "police," purporting to represent all departments nationwide when stories are actually distinct to individual agencies. When they are good stories, they reflect favorably on the profession. They reflect poorly on all of us when they are controversial or negative. This is where we start our journey, building the reputation and image that our police officers and law-abiding citizens deserve through the power of narration, sound bites, and community engagement. It's the beginning of mastering the art of strategic communication.

WHY IS THIS IMPORTANT?

Communicating when it matters or not communicating at all can mean the difference in job preservation, community trust, and keeping employees engaged. If you are like me, you may have wondered how we got to this point in policing. Why does it seem the news media always focuses on negative news stories surrounding cops? Why do police chiefs have such a short shelf life? How can some community members throw insults at the very officers who took an oath to protect them while others buy them lunches without them knowing? Why do some members of the public experience such disdain and hatred toward us that they burn our police cars or hurl objects at those sworn to protect them? What has happened to the level of trust that we previously enjoyed in this country? How did some symbols representing the nobility of policing get hijacked to mean extremism and division? Where do we go from here?

These questions continually arise at law enforcement conferences focusing on contemporary leadership issues. I get a lot of calls from agencies and executives when they feel the squeeze and are put into a negative situation in the community. The most common request I receive deals with managing the communications side of an incident or issue. All too often, executives are ill-prepared to deal with something as simple as talking to the media, releasing a fact set to the community, and messaging internally with their workforce. Strategic communication is the most important aspect that police executives often overlook.

What if I told you that your longevity as a sheriff or police chief depends on understanding and adhering to best practices in communication? For those of you who have either experienced this firsthand or witnessed one of your peers undergo this hard lesson, you would immediately raise your hand in agreement. A key reminder taught in leadership academies around the country is that leaders who cannot or are unwilling to communicate are just one major tragedy away from being on the unemployment line.

Strategic communication keeps your ship on course. When leaders are pushed out, especially during turbulent times, there is a harmful effect across the agency and profession. A cascade of negative news stories and community comments will likely follow a forced departure, undermining credibility and eroding trust in any agency and the profession.

HOW WELL DO WE COMMUNICATE?

There is a problem in American policing due to how officers have been trained to communicate. Historically, policing has typically been viewed as a secretive society—something that outsiders may refer to as an "us versus them" mentality. Police officers have been conditioned to think that the investigation takes precedence over everything else, including releasing any information we fear may derail a criminal inquiry. Unfortunately, this has resulted in countless law enforcement executives losing their jobs, communities in crisis, and officers left holding the bag to restore order and a sense of normalcy.

While no one advocates that agencies release too much information, best practices suggest that basic information be provided to answer questions that a community would legitimately be interested in. This is the balancing act of maintaining investigative integrity while subscribing to the basic tenets of informing the public. In policing, silence is not golden, as many were previously taught. It can have the opposite effect of speaking volumes or allowing people to fill in their own narration of what they believe occurred during incidents. "No comment" is a comment.

Look no further than to recent school shootings, officer misconduct incidents, horrific fires, and other critical incidents that captivate the minds and attention of those we swore an oath to protect and serve. Public information was often nonexistent, mistake-laden, or dribbled out like a leaking faucet. Information that is slow to be released harms an agency and the community and undermines credibility.

All these issues combine to create a perfect storm of misinformation and mistrust. There is no doubt that our people who don their badges, answer telephones, and provide core neighborhood services in the interest of public safety deserve better from our leaders. Our noble profession deserves better.

As leaders, we must commit ourselves to handling public information with excellence. We must strategize on the best way to manage communications. We must train what we would do if the unthinkable landed on our doorsteps.

This means obtaining factually based information in a timely manner. Everyone knows that knowledge of facts can evolve, especially during a critical incident, and that initial information may change as the incident unfolds. The real focus should be obtaining a basic fact set that can be released immediately. We train extensively in other aspects of policing, such as firearms proficiency, use of force, and emergency vehicle operation, however, we continually overlook the basics of releasing facts to the public, media, and our employees. Why is that?

I am not purporting that there is a conspiracy to cover up incidents, nor am I saying that these issues are intentional on the part of leaders. I believe most executives want to excel in their positions, emphasizing positive community engagement. I am advocating for reaffirming and committing to strategies that put our profession in the most effective position. Everyone knows it is much easier to police in communities that respect their departments. Have you ever wondered what the core foundation of building trust is? It's communication. It's being strategic about communication efforts.

Bottom line: we hire executives to lead police agencies of all shapes and sizes. We train them on budget, policy, and the inner workings of their governmental structure. Rarely do we formally strategize on how to communicate effectively. It's as if the profession assumes that communication will occur naturally. While some charismatic leaders possess a natural gift in oral and written communication, as professionals, we can no longer approach communication haphazardly and hope that our leaders will get through the tough times on their own. We must commit to learning, partnering with peers, attending leadership conferences, and investing in tools and strategies that work.

Additionally, the problem is that we are creatures of habit. For decades, we barely released details about an incident, or we hid behind the notion that we could not release video of an officer-involved shooting until the district attorney said we could. Some states indeed have very restrictive laws governing the release of public information. Some of us are stuck in the past and keep doing what we have always done—embracing a "nothing here to see or talk about" mentality. Some agencies have determined that their department will only push releases on social media, thereby bypassing traditional media. Ironically, we see a shift to removing the ability to comment on some posts. This is detrimental to our profession and will further erode public trust and continuing challenges for agencies.

Communication takes many different facets—internal, external, written, spoken, video-based, audio content, and social media. Police leaders cannot fully understand community perspectives without committing to getting communication right. Unsurprisingly, several successful law enforcement executives form community advisory boards, chiefs' panels, and consultative groups to stay in touch with the community's perceptions and mindset. By listening and actively participating in conversations, both internally and in external-facing groups, executives can become more informed, which leads to better decision-making across the board.

The saying "it's lonely at the top" can take on a new meaning, suggesting that the top may be the last person to know what is happening inside the organization or within the community. That is why leaders must formally commit themselves to communication practices and find ways to receive information from various sources.

One way for a leader to accomplish information gathering is to have the right people monitoring community social media posts, which can alert an agency that trouble, or perception of trouble, is brewing. The correct people can also produce content that meets the communication demands of the jurisdiction and can quickly release appropriate information. Best-selling author Jim Collins said it best: "Great vision without great people is irrelevant." His book *Good To Great* features a multitude of leadership principles for the private sector that also have significant relevance for governmental agencies[3]. Agency heads will learn how to ensure the right person is in the correct position to lead communication in the subsequent chapter.

STRATEGIC THINKING

What is strategic thinking? Leaders and communicators must embrace a way of receiving information, assessing it, formulating a plan, executing the strategy, and then evaluating their effectiveness. The acronym, modified slightly from military planners, is ACE:

- **ASSESS**
- **CHOOSE A PLAN**
- **EXECUTE AND EVALUATE**

It takes time to think strategically. When faced with a tough situation, I often place my iPhone into the "do not disturb" setting, empty my office of distractions and people, and clear my mind. First, I write out the problem or issue our team faces. Next, I jot down the objective and goal. This is the assessment and planning phase of strategic thinking.

Once comfortable, the next step is to choose a plan. The emphasis should be on considering all the alternatives, balancing risks and rewards, and planning the best possible solution. What will enable the highest likelihood for our team to reach the objective and goal? A decision is required, for better or worse. Indecisiveness will lead to communication failures. Even if the chosen path is wrong or miscalculated, there will be an additional phase to achieve success.

The last phase of strategic thinking is execution and evaluation. We chose our path; now, it's time to take it. Execution and evaluation can be a tangible series of steps. For example, suppose the decision was to host a press conference, release dashcam video, and bring in outside investigative agency support. The execution phase involves completing those tasks.

Many leaders who have taken my advice on the ACE strategy, including myself, sometimes forget to evaluate the effectiveness of the strategy. Occasionally, we get lucky and execute a brilliant strategy, lessening the desire to reconsider our plan. You are selling yourself short if you don't take some time to evaluate. The evaluation phase may be a formal process, such as an after-action report or simply informal notes placed in your go bag for future similar incidents.

Trust me on this. Strategic thinking will aid you in your career. I will go one step further: it will propel you through future career advancement. Strategic thinking improves your agency's response. It lessens rumors and misinformation. It builds trust, not only with the community and media but with your employees.

So, how do you start thinking strategically? It's a developed trait that must be intentional. With practice and commitment, you can develop your strategic thinking skill set. Once you adopt the ACE strategic principles, you can apply them in many facets of your professional and personal life. My marriage is better because of this premise. I have a better relationship with my city manager due to ACE thinking.

The sky is the limit on how you can embrace this concept. ACE will assist you with strategy development, from team planning and visionary roadmaps to forecasting future initiatives that are important to your agency. Strategic thinkers are accustomed to continually searching for improvement within their organizations. They anticipate problems. In doing so, responding to challenges becomes less stressful and easier to manage. Imagine having a strategy to deal with any obstacle as a police executive. Your current goals, mission, and vision statements should align with strategic thinking and communication strategies to put you in an advantageous position should any problem arise.

While on the topic of strategic thinking, it is appropriate to discuss risk-taking. Law enforcement is inherently a dangerous and risky business. Most police executives face litigation regularly. We adopt policies and practices to mitigate risks, but the very nature of our profession carries certain risks. A significant element of thinking strategically is assessing issues and problems, developing goals and plans to elevate community standing, and choosing a path that involves taking risks. Now, I am not talking about taking unnecessary risks. I am referencing encouraging our teams to innovate to solve problems.

For example, I was among the first executives to start a body-camera-of-the-week program in Arlington, Texas. It was innovative and bold. Most agencies could not imagine dumping footage, seemingly irrelevant, to the community without an open records or Freedom of Information Act (FOIA) request. But, it negated the community mindset that body camera footage always showed a negative interaction. At the time of this groundbreaking initiative, the only body camera videos being shown across Texas dealt with officer-involved shootings, officer misconduct, and police pursuits that typically resulted in major crashes.

Using the ACE strategic thinking template, we assessed the problem: communities believe we only shoot people, chase people in cars, and engage in misconduct, reinforced by those types of videos. Our goal was to showcase the everyday work of our officers—changing flat tires, responding to calls for service, unlocking people's cars, and so on. The plan was to find routine body camera footage that could be released weekly. Our chosen path was to brand the program as "APD Body Worn Camera of the Week" and distribute these videos across social media. We executed it with the assistance of our videographer and former television photojournalist, and the public loved this new initiative. It was out-of-the-box thinking at the time. We evaluated the effectiveness and made a few tweaks here and there.

Interestingly, something happened with the body camera video program we had not anticipated. The local broadcast media grabbed the videos from social media and profiled many of them. We moved the needle on public perception regarding capturing video and achieving our goals.

STRATEGIC COMMUNICATION

The next topic concerning the *why* deals with strategically communicating. Now that we know how to think strategically, how does this translate to communication? Strategic communication includes tools, principles, strategies, channels, and guiding plans to accomplish your goals and objectives. It reinforces the agency's mission, vision, and values. "Excellence In Everything We Do" is my agency's current vision statement. "Honor Above All, Service Before Self" was the vision statement at my prior agency. With these visionary statements, one can recognize, regardless of position or assignment, that the strategic principles of the organizations are embodied in these words.

Once you have developed your leadership strategy, gained through strategic thinking, the next action is to intertwine communication initiatives to further that strategy. It's about being intentional in your corporate communications. We need to have a plan. During critical incidents, there should be a written guidebook on what to say, how to say it, and how to protect your department's reputation. Strategic communication is about delegating tasks related to pushing information through various mediums and channels. Think of being strategic in your communications in the following manner:

- **YOU WANT TO PUSH THE BEST POSSIBLE MESSAGE.**
- **YOU WANT TO REACH YOUR DIFFERENT AUDIENCES.**
- **YOU WANT TO USE THE RIGHT CHANNELS.**
- **YOU WANT TO BE EASILY UNDERSTANDABLE.**
- **YOU WANT TO BE TIMELY AND RESPONSIVE.**
- **YOU WANT TO ENSURE YOUR MESSAGING REFLECTS YOUR ORGANIZATIONAL VALUES, MISSION, AND VISION.**

Anyone can communicate for the sake of communicating. Being purposeful with a plan requires diligence and work. This is what differentiates being strategic in communications from just spewing information. As Simon Sinek points out, "We are drawn to leaders and organizations that are good at communicating what they believe. Their ability to make us feel like we belong, to make us feel special, safe, and not alone is part of what gives them the ability to inspire us."[4]

WHY ENGAGE WITH MEDIA

The media's power to influence and reflect public opinion has become more pronounced since the dot-com boom. Leveraging traditional and social media can position agencies to collaborate better with community members.[5] Law enforcement executives can better message their agencies in the chosen desired form and fashion.

I will never forget a lunch meeting with an executive from a midsize agency. The conversation centered on the executive's department not embracing social media or seeing the value in communicating with traditional media. While intently listening to his misguided attempts to justify not communicating, I was intrigued by the thinking. I couldn't help wondering how many other agency executives are in the same boat as this guy. While the conversation continued with pleasantries and ended with the pointed question of whether I believed that their agency was headed in the wrong direction as it related to managing public information, I was quietly performing social media searches on my telephone to demonstrate that regardless of whether their agency embraced social media or not, the community was already engaging in many conversations about their team on several different platforms. The chief was taken aback. In the course of a lunch conversation, I had managed to change the mind of this executive.

Traditional media remains relevant in our society. Even in small-town America, news media may cover events and incidents. It's important to note that we can leverage their reach to bolster our strategic goals. Even in times of adversity, media can assist with conveying the facts.

Through the advent of social media, law enforcement continues to be at the forefront of both the good and the bad. Heroic videos of pulling crash victims from a burning car will reinforce the notion that police are here to help. Arresting a serious offender highlights to the community that we provide a valuable and noteworthy service. Asking for the public to assist our teams in identifying a prolific burglar reinvigorates the notion that it takes the community to participate and provide tips to solve crimes. Posting a photograph of a newly hired officer and why they joined our profession will human-ize our career field.

On the other end of the spectrum, that use of force inci-dent uploaded to YouTube may question your agency's tac-tics and how the agency polices. A rant by an upset mom on the status of an investigation about her daughter may be viewed as legitimate in the eyes of social media beholders. Throw in an officer misconduct case, and agencies will likely be forced into a dialogue surrounding the issues. Worse yet, imagine your agency being blamed for the misfortunes of another agency. These examples happen more frequently than one would imagine. And, in recent times, deadly force encounters have called into question the whole legitimacy of our profession.

While many of these facets can put a damper on the future outlook of policing, I think they provide unique opportuni-ties to better influence our narratives. *The Art Of Strategic Communication* seeks to do just that—present new ideas and enable executives to leverage traditional media and harness the power of social media, video, and audio platforms to remain the authoritative source for your organization.

MESSAGING TRIANGLE

Dr. Theron Bowman, an accomplished scholar and police chief, posited a messaging triangle for executives.[6] At its basic core, we should try to frame communication efforts into the following groups.

The triangle has the community at the top point. Employ-ees are on the left anchor, while bosses (city managers, may-ors, and elected officials) are on the right anchor. It would be great if we could keep all three groups engaged and happy with our comms strategy. Still, leaders must always have at least two groups in their corner regarding a communications strategy to reduce the likelihood of trouble.

Dr. Bowman coached that sometimes our messaging may not resonate with employees, however, as long as we had the community and our bosses on our side, we would likely survive the messaging. Similarly, if our messaging strategy agitated the bosses, as long as employees and the community were in our corner, we would probably be OK. Lastly, if the community questioned our messaging but we had the employees and bosses behind us, we would generally be all right.

This is not a scientific experiment that will reign true in every situation; however, I view it as a guidepost to consider when making large, sometimes difficult, decisions that affect the agency, community, and leadership teams. I incorporate it into my strategic thinking and communication strategies. It has also been a great reminder that if my communications strategy pitted two of the three groups against me, I better rethink the strategy and messages or face an uphill battle that may turn bad.

Using the strategic thinking template of ACE, draw a triangle during your assessment and planning phase. This will help you avoid choosing a plan that does not elicit the necessary support that may be needed during the execution phase.

AUDIENCES

There are ten probable audiences that your team will deal with. Crafting the appropriate message to your audiences should not be a one-size-fits-all approach. If you are a police chief, your messaging to your city manager or mayor/city council should look different than the standard news release that goes to everyone. Yes, you probably should include the release of the notification to your boss. Still, you should also have some high-level comments to frame the conversation with elected officials and bosses. This is one example of why knowing your target audience as a leader is important.

Here are the ten potential audiences:

1. **PRO-POLICE CROWD**—These folks love you, even when times are tough. They are your biggest cheerleaders. However, this is not the audience we usually need to reach since their mindset aligns with our agencies.

2. **EVERYDAY CITIZENS**—These are the people who are typically in your corner. Historically, most citizens support the idea of rule and law and that policing provides a vital service, even though our profession has experienced some recent hits to trust. Also, leaders and advisors need to understand that the level of support can vary across racial and ethnic backgrounds due to historical precedence and high-profile incidents. Our messaging focus should spend much time and effort with the everyday citizen.

3. **ANTI–LAW ENFORCEMENT CROWD**—For whatever reason, these individuals typically do not support policing initiatives. It could be a bad experience they had or a multitude of other reasons. Don't give up on trying to make positive inroads by demonstrating the care and service your team provides. If you encounter this audience, there are times that a reasonable discussion may be able to turn a person to see a positive point of view surrounding law enforcement. Put a lot of effort into trying to change minds and perceptions based upon earning their respect and trust, which could be a long road, but worth it to put someone in your agency's corner.

4. **HATERS**—People who hate law enforcement. Unlike the anti–law enforcement crowd, which may be able to be swayed toward the middle or even into a supportive role, these folks typically are set in their mind and will work to stir trouble at every turn. If your team meets with them and it's evident that they are in this category, it may be best to try to ignore their social media rants or comments made in public. Unfortunately, I have seen many leaders try to reset a hater, only to be taken advantage of when the time is right. We still provide professional service to this group—we just don't put a lot of energy into messaging this type of audience. The good news is that

haters are small in numbers, and your supporters can sometimes drown out their voices.

5. **TROLLS**—The old saying "don't feed the trolls" applies to communication. These are typically your haters who like to bait the agency in meetings or on social media. Avoid contact where you can, and treat them with kindness and professionalism if you must engage.

6. **YOUR EMPLOYEES**—Leaders and strategic communication advisors must realize that employees are also an audience. Make no mistake—when leaders take the podium to speak during a news conference, employees listen and will have opinions.

7. **NEIGHBORING LAW ENFORCEMENT AGENCIES**—In every agency I have worked in, there is a certain level of competitiveness with other agencies, from who can pay the best salaries and gets the most positive media coverage to who has the coolest gadgets and programs. Based upon this, assume that your neighboring agencies are watching your communication efforts—which is expected and may be viewed as a strategic mindset to stay abreast of what is happening. This also means that you don't talk about another agency unless you get permission from their leader and can do it in a way that reflects favorably on them.

8. **ELECTED OFFICIALS AND BOSSES**—As a leader and strategic advisor, we can't lose sight of our elected officials, city managers, county commissioners, district attorneys, and other important people who are astutely watching our communications. We must ensure we are messaging appropriately and making notifications before this audience sees it on television.

9. **NEWS MEDIA**—The media is an audience. This book has strategies for maximizing your key messages and sound bites to this audience.

10. **RETIREES, FAMILIES OF YOUR EMPLOYEES, AND FORMER EMPLOYEES**—While these three groups get lumped into the last audience category, your goal is to keep them on your side. A disgruntled retiree or former employee who resigned or was terminated can cause a stir on the communications side. Families can also be a force multiplier as your team highlights the positive work being accomplished by their loved ones.

LAYOUT OF BOOK

The topics are laid out straightforwardly. The table of contents was strategically developed as a reference that one can quickly flip to, depending on the situation your agency is facing. Based on extensive experience in public and media relations coupled with countless hours with tenured colleagues at educational conferences, this book serves as a testament to those who have come before us and those who will uphold best practices that make a better profession and more informed community. Blueprints are included at the end of each chapter. When appropriate, checklists are included that allow one to quickly reference important considerations when your agency is in the "thick of it."

REINFORCING THE "WHY"

Why should law enforcement leaders care about strategic communications, media relations, and public engagement? Some may think we have never had anything occur in our jurisdiction that would warrant media training or attention. Or better yet, the news media leaves us alone, right? Wrong. In the twenty-first century, we have seen law enforcement agencies all too often cast into public scrutiny based on one of their officer's alleged or actual actions. For good or bad, this is where we are as a society—something occurs, and now this incident is placed before your bosses and their bosses for the whole community or the entire world to see.

Therefore, getting things right is important. What happens on the West Coast can directly affect the East Coast and vice versa. We no longer live in a world where news coverage stays localized. Depending on the type and magnitude of an incident, news can break across regions and even the entire country. Judy Pal, a good friend and mentor, recently reported that about a third of crises go international within one hour.[7] Let that statistic sink in for a minute. In that initial hour, there is probably no way that you have time to gather all the credible facts and create a messaging strategy or employ the ACE strategic thinking template. As an agency, you are already starting behind the curve.

There were many times in my career when I had been driving to a call, and before I even arrived, my telephone was blowing up with reporters and news desks calling to get the inside scoop. It doesn't matter what size agency you work for. I have worked at small, medium, and large agencies. Depending on the type of incident, any department can become the center of an intense news story. Pretending that nothing is going on will not work and will ultimately lead to the demise of your credibility and possibly your career.

I am not conveying that every big story becomes a problem, nor am I indicating that every big story is negative. However, we respond to shootings, robberies, and other violent crime incidents that typically generate news inquiries and public interest. Advertising dollars drive the commercial nature of traditional news organizations. They compete with other news outlets in their quest to be number one. Crime, controversy, and conflict are well-represented topics in a typical newscast.

In some cases, a school shooting, even if no one is seriously injured or killed, may cause national news. A use of force incident that a community member films may appear on the evening news solely based on the captured video, with no regard to the appropriateness of the application of force. Many people are looking for an opportunity to become that next social media sensation with a viral video that involves police. In all cases that take center stage, public information should take precedence over other job responsibilities to ensure we prioritize messaging correctly. We have other team members who can take care of the investigative aspects, evidence collection, and scene processing. As executives, we must be dialed into strategic thinking, strategic planning, and strategic communication.

Taking public relations and information management seriously is vital to your success. Regardless of the size of your police department, someone needs to be prepared to handle incidents that arise. This book will help you with best practices that have been developed over decades of experience. Managing news stories and messaging directly to your community members is one of the most important aspects for any contemporary law enforcement agency.

Remember when you saw a breaking news event unfolding on television or social media. If you are like me, you can think of some agencies that commanded the scene and projected confidence in their ability. I bet you can also think of some incidents where the agency was either nonresponsive or went to the microphones unprepared. This spells disaster, overemphasizing the incident and placing scrutiny on whoever is in charge. Questions about your readiness and capability become prevalent. For example, within days of the horrific Maui wildfires that destroyed the town of Lahaina and claimed many lives, the head of the emergency management agency was out, mainly due to communication challenges.[8] Mismanagement of communications can lead to your failure, not to mention the needless stress you must endure.

By its very nature, law enforcement lends itself to curiosity, with the public having an instinctive desire to know what is happening. We must develop our skill sets to message our communities and work alongside reporters and citizen journalists. I want this book to be a valuable resource you can access whenever needed. The information is based on real-life incidents and experiences, not hypotheticals. Many lessons were born out of high-profile incidents that forever changed me as a police officer. By their very nature, the big incidents are the ones we need to get correct from the start.

BLUEPRINT—CHAPTER 1

STRATEGIC THINKING ACE TEMPLATE

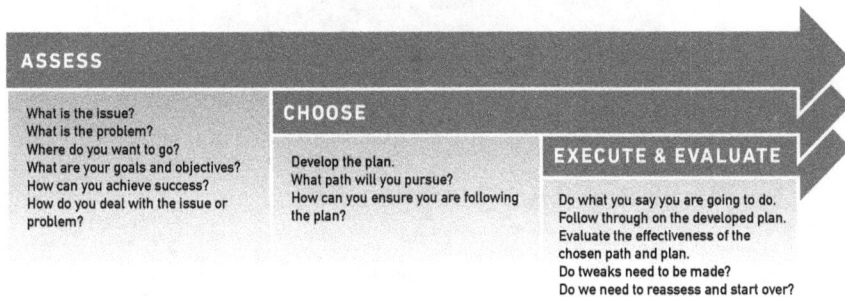

ASSESS

What is the issue?
What is the problem?
Where do you want to go?
What are your goals and objectives?
How can you achieve success?
How do you deal with the issue or problem?

CHOOSE

Develop the plan.
What path will you pursue?
How can you ensure you are following the plan?

EXECUTE & EVALUATE

Do what you say you are going to do.
Follow through on the developed plan.
Evaluate the effectiveness of the chosen path and plan.
Do tweaks need to be made?
Do we need to reassess and start over?

STRATEGIC COMMUNICATION PARADIGM

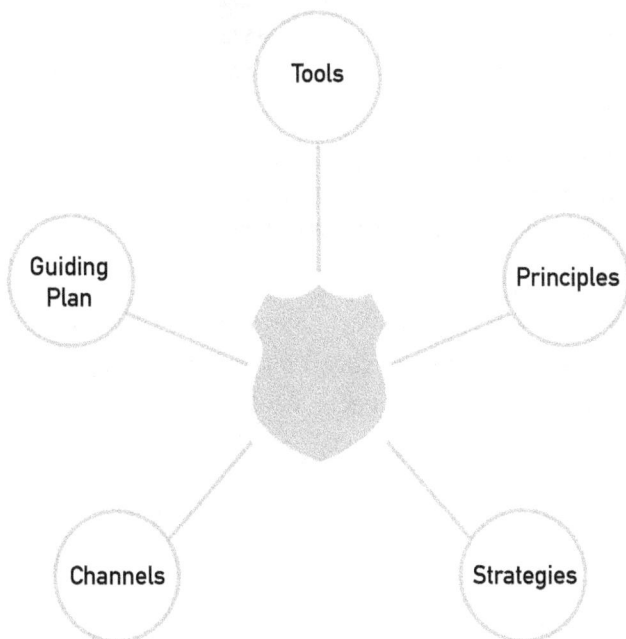

Tools

Guiding Plan

Principles

Channels

Strategies

MESSAGING TRIANGLE

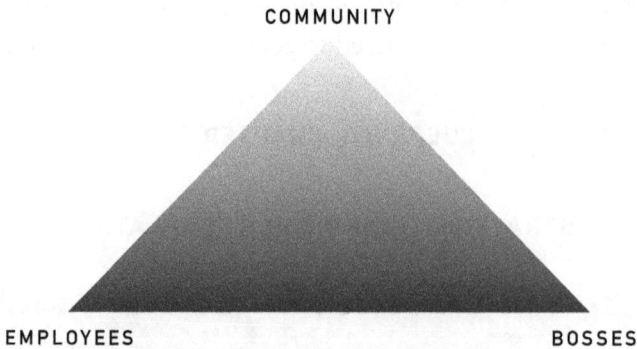

COMMUNITY

EMPLOYEES   BOSSES

CHAPTER 1 PRO TIPS

- Communication is the core foundation for success in an agency.

- Strategic thinking involves the ACE principle—Assess, Choose, Execute, and Evaluate.

- Strategic communication encompasses the tools, principles, strategies, channels, and guiding plan to accomplish your goals and objectives in alignment with your agency's mission, vision, and values.

- The messaging triangle serves as a check and balance to ensure you generate support for your communication decisions—balancing community, employees, and bosses.

While there are many different audiences, leaders and strategic communication advisors/PIOs must tailor specific messaging to each target audience.

CHAPTER 2

DON'T BURY THE LEDE

In 2012, training was held in Vancouver, Canada. The theme centered on sharpening your message through a new communication tool slowly being adopted in police agencies— social media. Yes, I know the origins of social media for the rest of humanity started much earlier, but remember, government changes at a snail's pace. In addition, there were a lot of unknowns and potential risks with this new communication network. Many executives were uninterested in trying something new or didn't want to rock the boat.

A trailblazer, Lauri Stevens, well-known internationally as a social media strategist, was spreading the word about how social media would improve law enforcement, crime prevention, and officer safety. She founded the "Social Media the Internet and Law Enforcement" (SMILE) Conference to do just that. In addition to her own proficiency, Lauri always had a knack for booking influential speakers who were experts in their field.

During the sessions, I met Anne E. Schwartz, best-selling author and law enforcement consultant, along with Sean Whitcomb, a sergeant with the Seattle Police Department at the time. These chance encounters led to innovative thought surrounding strategic communication. Presenters from across the US and Canada talked about how law enforcement was on the cusp of something great with this new tool.

Social media will forever change communication. Agencies could be proactive. Departments could zero in on their sound bites and message directly to communities, bypassing traditional methods. As Anne and Sean agreed, not only did we need to put the important information at the front of our messaging, but agencies needed to convey a call to action to increase public safety through citizen engagement. Communication advisors demanded a seat at the executive table, with less chain of command to get in the way of developing and posting content. Many modern-day practices started with emphasizing critical information at the front—news releases, social media, and storytelling.

DON'T BURY THE LEDE

"Burying the lede," a journalism term that originated in the 1970s, means placing the most essential information in the middle of a story—not the beginning. This can lead to confusion and the failure of community members to take some requested action, prevent people from even reading your story, and may eventually lead to mistrust. This is the second part of the *why* related to thinking and communicating strategically.

If you are dealing with a train derailment that could release hazardous gases, here is an example of where the lede is buried: communication that provides the news of a train derailment, stating there are some road closures in the area. On the other hand, with the lede up front, strategic communication would place a call to action at the beginning of the messaging: "Citizens around Main Street and Center Street need to evacuate immediately due to a train derailment. Out of an abundance of caution, traffic in the area has been diverted to

Second Street as first responders evaluate the contents of the train cars involved. For safety reasons, immediately evacuate these areas and follow all instructions from first responders. An update will be provided once more information is known and can be shared." Do you see the difference?

As executives and communicators, we must determine the most important information that must be readily available and shared with community members and employees. By placing this information at the beginning of a news briefing, at the top of a news release, and in a social media post, we put the lede front and center to quickly convey the most important aspects of strategic communication.

Agencies should include a call to action in the messaging. What do you want the public to do? Shelter in place? Just be aware of the incident? Evacuate? Provide tips? The call to action is important because it empowers your community to participate. This reinforces your messaging because the recipient will better understand what to do.

Some departments may want to consider using a hook. This refers to posting an attention-grabbing headline encouraging people to click on a message. From a public safety perspective, hooks are not always needed, as followers are generally interested in what a law enforcement agency has to say. But a hook may serve its intended purpose. Don't create a hook, however, that exaggerates the importance of the topic at hand.

It is important who you choose to manage communications. Even in midsize to large agencies that have a dedicated spokesperson, there will be times when it is appropriate for the chief executive to handle communications. An example would be a situation where an officer has been seriously injured or killed. The public and employees want to hear from the boss—not the spokesperson, assistant chief, or captain— they want the boss.

HOW I ENDED UP AS A CHIEF SPOKESPERSON

I graduated from the police academy almost thirty years ago, so some may refer to me as an "old head." Like most young officers, I made my rounds in various positions, including patrol, traffic enforcement, and drug interdiction, before being promoted through the ranks. The furthest thing from my mind was that somehow, I would end up the chief spokesperson for a major metropolitan police department or, eventually, a police chief.

I received a phone call in 2011 with the voice on the other end directing me to report to the media office upon my return from vacation. Initially, I was not excited about leaving a highway drug interdiction unit as a sergeant. At the time, the militarization of policing conversation had come full circle, and domestic highway enforcement units were under the microscope. As any agile career-minded individual would do, I reported as instructed. This journey started my career path in police-media-community relations.

Furthermore, my path would intersect with three of the largest law enforcement-communication groups in the world: the International Association of Chiefs of Police Public Information Officers Section, the Major Cities Chiefs Association Public Information Officers Committee, and the National Information Officers Association. As a chair and president, I had the great opportunity to lead all three of these storied organizations. This culminated in lifelong friendships, but more importantly, it built a solid core of trusted advisors where ideas could be bounced around, and help could be solicited when times were tough. This is the real value of joining organizations: to expand your network and learn best practices. Networking with peers and communication professionals is a core competency for any good leader and spokesperson.

We all have our stories of how we arrived at our positions. Some of you may be in a small agency where there is no need for a dedicated spokesperson. That duty likely will fall to you as a leader, chief executive, or sheriff. Others may work in a medium-sized agency where the recruiter doubles as a public information officer when needed. Those who work in even larger agencies may have a dedicated person responsible for dealing with the media and carrying the organization's message. In the largest agencies, you may even be a part of a team of professionals tasked with all aspects of communications. Regardless of your agency's size, you will need to speak to the media and public at some point when the news is not always flattering. Also, a commitment to communicating strategically is paramount. This requires you, a person, or a team of individuals to perform those duties. Imagine this for a moment. Your department may be the very best in the world. It may have the best people doing a great job. But if someone is not telling or sharing their story, it does not matter how good the people are or how well the agency is performing because no one has awareness.

When I received my first appointment as police chief, I inherited a good agency. There were no outwardly facing major problems. However, inside, there was a lot of friction, resulting in a lack of communication. There was a lack of trust between the rank and file and the upper echelon. Sound familiar? This is a common problem, as recent studies show that communication is one of the biggest obstacles between executives and line personnel.[9]

As I eased into the agency, I made it a priority to fix the internal communications. Once we made progress on that endeavor, I started showcasing the excellent police work being done. We utilized videos, podcasts, news releases, press conferences, and a whole range of social media photos and stories to demonstrate the immense value of the team to the community. The feedback was overwhelmingly positive—the perceptions were that the agency, under new leadership, was now working harder than ever. This is what's interesting about this story. The team was doing what they always did, with one major difference. Now, they had a leader who knew how to profile their work. The story was getting out. Public trust was increasing. Employees were vying to be the next officer to make the big crime bust or receive the community accolades that could be shared on social media. It was an amazing time to see the smiles on officers who had never been publicly thanked before. That's why strategic thinking and communication is extremely important.

WHAT IS A STRATEGIC COMMUNICATION ADVISOR/PIO?

A PIO may be called by several different titles and wear many distinctive hats. An emerging trend refers to a PIO as a strategic communications advisor (this is appealing—as it reflects on the job functions this book advocates for). They may be called a public relations officer, media strategist, communications specialist, videographer, social media coordinator, podcast host, graphics artist, or other similar titles. They may be sworn or nonsworn. They may be trained journalists or come from your rank and file. They may possess an advanced degree or have a high school diploma. They may have other primary duties.

Regardless of who you choose or what you call it, even if that falls to you, the contemporary PIO should be responsible for the dissemination of facts and information, the development of goals and objectives through a strategic communication and crisis plan, and innovation in telling your agency's story proactively. Duties will need to include graphic design, video-based products, audio storytelling, social media engagement, writing news releases, conducting interviews, building and maintaining positive relationships with traditional media, marketing the agency, protecting brand integrity, publishing reports, overseeing the website, monitoring media stories, and guiding internal communication; the list goes on and on.

Don't fret if you haven't even considered appointing someone to this role yet. I would argue that this puts you in a great position. Selecting a communications person or assigning important duties related to communications is one of the most essential decisions you will make as a leader. Your communications professional will be the expert to lead the agency through many issues. This advisor will need to possess impeccable integrity and be able to engage in strategic thinking processes to connect with employees and the community. This person will be your trusted confidant and allowed in the inner circle of the executive command staff. They must be comfortable presenting alternate solutions that may directly conflict with what you, as a leader, may be thinking. The decision is yours and yours alone, but your advisor should not be afraid to challenge groupthink based on their educational credentials, experience, and networks. From a strategic communication standpoint, this PIO must be brutally honest, leveraging insights from ACE strategic thinking.

WHERE ARE WE HEADED?

As Zig Ziglar most eloquently said, "If you want to reach a goal, you must 'see the reaching' in your own mind before you actually arrive at your goal."[10] Internally, people like to know where the ship is heading. Good communication will help an executive and agency define the path forward. A clear roadmap for your strategy should include how the public information position will be established and reported.

Department leaders need to develop an ability to overcome obstacles. When studying business, Jim Collins determined overcoming obstacles was a key factor in greatness.[11] It has been my experience that most "obstacles" require some level of communication—albeit some more than others—internally, externally, or both.

Whether you have a dedicated employee who will solely perform the public information role or an employee who will have those duties as the need arises, do yourself a huge favor and follow this advice: the employee, without exception, should be a direct report to the head of the agency. This also goes for anyone developing social media posts, strategies, video content, and anything else for the agency's platforms, including the website.

The employee needs direct and unfettered access to the top leadership position in the department to allow the employee to discuss sensitive topics honestly and strategize how to navigate adverse incidents best. In addition, it will enable the employee to hear the leader's point of view firsthand. The public information officer is a direct extension of the agency head. When they speak, this, in turn, represents the leader and agency.

Chuck Wexler, executive director for the Police Executive Research Forum, reiterates the importance of picking good people as fundamental for leaders.[12] I would argue one step further: choosing the right person to lead communications is crucial for the modern-day law enforcement executive. This person is an extension of the chief executive officer—you. Treat this selection and appointment with the careful consideration it deserves to increase the likelihood of future success. Remember, the reputation and standing of your agency depend on how well a communications advisor can perform.

Why is any of this relevant? Simply put, the employee assigned to deal with the media, manage your social media platforms, and create products that resonate positively with your community needs to be directly under the leader on the organizational chart. It is that important. Having a myriad of layers, cumbersome bureaucracies, and extensive chain of command will undoubtedly stifle decision-making, timely responses, and innovation. On the contrary, strategic communication advisors that can speak to the boss, as needed, will be in a positive position to quickly conduct assessments, plan strategies, and execute mission objectives as it relates to communication activities.

IMPORTANCE OF RIGHT FIT

There are a few positions within a police department that are vital for the success of executives. One is the strategic communications advisor/public information officer. You can look across the country and see the failures that affected police chiefs' careers. Often, there was a miscalculation on the importance of dealing with the media and engaging with community stakeholders. A good, well-trained advisor/public information officer can influence public outcomes through proven strategies. They can tap into a network of professionals who work together for the greater good of the profession. Right fit means someone who meshes well with you. Ensure the individual works well with your leadership style and is aligned with your vision and goals.

SELECTION PROCESS

Let us assume you plan to appoint someone (standalone duty or ancillary role) as media-public liaison. They should be someone you trust immensely, who can present differing viewpoints and not be afraid to argue about possible paths for consideration. You do not want a "yes person" who always agrees with the chief executive. Being a critical thinker, exploring several possibilities, and weighing the good and the bad are strong attributes in this role. While the chief executive ultimately will decide on communications direction, the advisor/public information officer has a duty and responsibility to present all alternatives, weighing the pros and cons, risks, and potential benefits.

Discussions between the CEO and the advisor/public information officer should be confidential. For medium-sized and large agencies, one point of contact should serve as the conduit and direct report to the chief executive while leading the overall media and public relations team. Having a department without someone trained to deal with media or message your community is like having a sailboat without a sail. It is necessary and important.

I have seen several agencies allow the proverbial ivory tower to get in the way of getting things done. For example, one large agency had a sergeant who reported to a lieutenant, who reported to a captain, who reported to an assistant chief—you get the point. Too much intermediary brass will impede good decisions and accomplishing your agency's goals. Things move fast, so this trusted advisor needs to act quickly, including communicating directly with the boss when needed.

I get this question a lot from chiefs while teaching at various conferences: should I hire a former news reporter or use someone in-house to serve in a public information officer role? While there is no one-size-fits-all approach, the question centers on what you are trying to accomplish. How much demand is there from local media in your community? What is the size of your agency? Do you have the capacity to have someone in-house transition into the role as necessary? How do you want to connect with residents, visitors, and business leaders? What are your short-term and long-term goals related to community policing initiatives? What level of engagement is appropriate for your constituents? What about your elected officials and senior city management?

While there is some disagreement in the communications landscape, I believe the real answer lies in the person appointed to the role. I have seen police officers perform at the highest level and outperform some civilian counterparts. I have also seen police officers botch the assignment completely, necessitating hiring an outside person with educational credentials and journalism experience to improve the office. Don't believe it has to be a police officer or it has to be a civilian—that thinking pushes you off course.

MY PERSONAL EXPERIENCE

When I was in my role as a deputy police chief overseeing the communications team in Arlington, Texas, I had a team of individuals who worked in support of our strategic communications. I hired both sworn and civilian team members. I had three former news reporters, a news producer, and a sports reporter who all worked on my team over the years. They brought a unique perspective that undeniably helped our agency through tough times.

When you bring an outsider in, the law enforcement culture can be unforgiving. To put these individuals in the best position for success, you must convey from day one that they are important hires. To fully immerse them into the agency, I would always have former journalists sit at the command staff table to further project my confidence to sworn members and to demonstrate their influence and importance to our organization.

Based on their previous roles in journalism, our agency was well-positioned with the media when pitching positive stories and responding to inquiries. This does not mean that sworn officers have no place in public information. On the contrary, I took the approach that each member brought their strengths to the team. Many stories within our strategic plan included putting a "uniform" on camera or pitching a story with police officers to project the humanistic side of policing.

Whether hiring an outsider or someone from the inside, it is imperative that they receive training. The sworn officer will need media training on proactively telling an agency's story. The outsider will need training on the ins and outs of policing. They must fully immerse themselves in the organization's culture. So when an executive asks me the proverbial question, sworn or civilian, my answer is always the same— both can do a great job if properly trained and allowed to innovate.

Regardless of whether you have a dedicated person, someone with "as assigned" duties, or a team to manage public affairs, the most important consideration is to select someone who wants to do the job and has a high level of competency to meet the work demands. This is not the typical 9 to 5 with weekends off kind of job. Inquiries can come in at all hours of the day and night. Incidents can happen on holidays. The public deserves to see content throughout the entire week. And messages come in on social media frequently.

In the new role, the person should understand that there will be late-night notifications, after-hours media inquiries, and responses on weekends. We do not get to control when the next shooting will occur. This does not mean that our personal lives are put on hold forever; it just means getting prepared for the expectations that the job will inevitably demand. Knowing these nuisances from the beginning will allow for maintaining a proper work-life balance.

While I admit I hesitated when initially moving into the spokesperson role, my fears were allayed after getting comfortable with the new assignment. It takes time to develop a natural groove between the boss and the advisor/spokesperson: learning how to write for the leader, speak for the leader, and carry out the goals and objectives of the agency. I remind police executives that the first year of being a strategic communications advisor/PIO is about getting to know the leader and developing trust between the two.

OTHER ATTRIBUTES TO CONSIDER
WHEN SELECTING YOUR ADVISOR/PIO

Creativity is also an important attribute to consider when looking for someone to take on this role. There will be many days when the advisor/public information officer needs to go back to the drawing table to strategize how they will assist the agency in reaching diverse audiences. They may need to identify communication gaps across the jurisdiction and find opportunities for and threats to the agency's brand and reputation.

Through creative approaches, products can be revolutionized to support the department's vision and values. How a social media post is written, a public report is produced, and a video is edited influence how community members interpret the information and support the agency's goals. To get people to participate in policing, creativity should be a priority in content development.

Being savvy with social media is also a plus. While training can get someone comfortable with the functionality of social platforms, it is important to have a mindset to seek meaningful public interactions through social media. I remember a funny story when a respected police chief met with me to say they were having issues getting their social media presence going. It quickly became evident that they had the wrong person in the position. The chief had appointed someone with the mindset that social media was not helpful for the policing profession; therefore, little energy was devoted to its use.

While technical skills are important, don't forget the soft skill sets. Learning media terminology and how a news cycle works is important. While I see many schools focus on interviewing techniques and how to write a news release, soft skills are just as important, such as proper etiquette when writing an email or answering a telephone call from a news station, having tough conversations with journalists, and presenting a disagreeing point of view to your boss and other leaders. These skills are crucial to your success as a leader and serving your boss well as a communicator.

NETWORKING

Encourage your PIO to continually learn and build a vast network of professionals who can assist in times of need. Many areas of the country have formal public information officer groups. Becoming involved in the latest trends and staying current with best practices is important as a law enforcement leader. The National Information Officers Association represents governmental communicators and hosts an annual conference on case studies and contemporary issues confronting PIOs and agencies. The International Association of Chiefs of Police (IACP) boasts a healthy public information officers section that includes many police chiefs. The IACP Public Information Officers Section typically hosts a midyear and annual conference. Most states also have communicator organizations. The goal is to train and learn at these conferences and build a professional network of peers that can be contacted for help. There is no shame in asking for assistance. This is what our profession needs: people who are not afraid to seek advice and replicate best practices during tough times.

FACTS—SYSTEM FOR MANAGING A CRISIS
OR CRITICAL INCIDENT AND TELLING STORIES

For any of you old enough to remember Sergeant Joe Friday, played by Jack Webb on the 1950s TV series *Dragnet* (if you don't know, that's OK too, just do a quick internet search), he had a particular saying, often misquoted, that enthralled the audience. "All we want are the facts, ma'am."[13] I want to focus on the word "facts," which should serve as the foundation for everything we do regarding communication. Without embellishment or exaggeration, we must operate in a land of facts. Credibility is key; once someone loses it, they are pretty much worthless in the eyes of the media and public.

The acronym that will be used throughout this book to assist you in managing a crisis or critical incident or for storytelling is FACTS. Sorry if your mind pictures Sergeant Joe Friday at your scenes; it is meant to help you develop your own protocols to manage a critical incident successfully. This is not to be confused with our ACE strategic thinking principles. ACE is about "thinking," and FACTS is about "communicating."

- **F**orecast
- **A**ssess
- **C**oordinate
- **T**ell your story
- **S**ocial media

Forecast deals with initial processes. It could be immediately following notification of an incident, and you are driving to a scene, and you run plausible scenarios through your mind. It could also be a new initiative that your department is launching, and you are forecasting what might be needed and timing.

Assess is what you do after you get on the scene. You are assessing to gather basic information on what is happening. The goal is to build a basic fact set that can be publicly shared with local media and your community.

Coordinate among you, the incident commander, investigative units, and your boss. You coordinate the information release to ensure that guilty knowledge information (facts only the perpetrator would know, for folks not in law enforcement) is not accidentally shared. You are also coordinating timing related to news conferences and press releases.

Tell your story is perhaps one of the most important aspects of the FACTS system. It could be walking toward a bank of cameras and providing a media briefing. It could also be a community meeting or a news release. The takeaway is that this is your opportunity to tell your story.

Social media is about reinforcing your story to those not present during the media briefing or meeting. It's about harnessing the power of social media to message your community. It can also be a call to action.

The FACTS system is an easy way to manage just about anything thrown your way. One of the benefits of having a system is that regardless of how stressful the event or incident is, you will remember the key aspects of creating the appropriate messaging.

BLUEPRINT—CHAPTER 2
FACTS METHOD OF STRATEGIC COMMUNICATION

INTERVIEW CHECKLIST
FOR HIRING A STRATEGIC COMMUNICATION ADVISOR
OR PUBLIC INFORMATION OFFICER

What experience do they have in strategic communications, public relations, branding, and journalism?

If choosing a sworn officer, are they respected by their teammates? What level of charisma do they possess? Sometimes, the public will want to see a uniform on social media and television during incidents.

If hiring a nonsworn staff member, what aptitude do they have for learning new concepts? For example, as a leader, you can teach them about policing practices if they don't come from a policing background. But be careful about selecting someone simply because they worked in journalism. While being a reporter or part of a news organization may provide some skill sets and relationships that they bring to the table, journalists may not possess skill sets that deal with the overall communication strategies or public relations that may be needed at the agency. The bottom line is that they must commit to being open and learning this side of the business.

What are their public speaking skills? Can they think fast on their feet? What are their writing skills? How creative are they? What about photo skills, video skills, editing, social media background, and visual storytelling?

Is this individual trustworthy? Can you confide in them the inner workings of the agency? Will they tell you when you are wrong? Can they analyze situations and advocate for their position? Behind closed doors, can you have candid conversations about the direction and strategy concerning an incident?

Can they work as a team player? Are they willing to check their ego at the door? The role can be in the limelight, but it's not about them. It's about the chief executive and agency.

What are their work habits and productivity levels? This position can be fast-paced and demanding. Are they willing to put forth the energy to monitor social media, even after hours and on weekends? Can they respond to scenes?

What is their ability to develop key relationships in the organization? As the chief executive, you need access to unfiltered information. More importantly, through strong relationships, your communications professional can learn positive things about the agency that can be highlighted.

Can they think outside of the box? Are they up on the latest trends and media savvy? Can they incorporate monitoring strategies that replicate best practices across the profession? Will they be able to network with peer agencies? What about their willingness to engage across the United States through formal public information officer groups?

Are they willing to put up with the highs and lows of dealing with the many facets of governmental communication? Can they remain objective and professional in their responses? Can they strategize innovative ways to reach diverse audiences?

RECOMMENDED ORGANIZATIONAL CHART

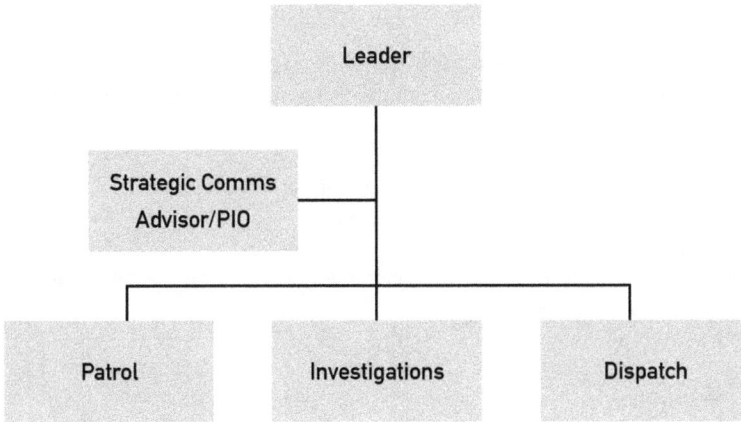

```
                        ┌──────────────┐
                        │    Leader    │
                        └──────┬───────┘
    ┌──────────────────┐      │
    │ Strategic Comms  │──────┤
    │   Advisor/PIO    │      │
    └──────────────────┘      │
        ┌─────────────────────┼─────────────────────┐
  ┌──────────┐        ┌──────────────┐        ┌──────────┐
  │  Patrol  │        │Investigations│        │ Dispatch │
  └──────────┘        └──────────────┘        └──────────┘
```

STRATEGIC PEER CONNECTION GUIDE—
NATIONAL ORGANIZATIONS

National Information Officers Association	www.nioa.org	865.389.8736 info@nioa.org
International Association of Chiefs of Police— Public Information Officers Section	www.theiacp.org	1.800.THE.IACP membership@theiacp.org
Major Cities Chiefs Association— Public Information Officers Committee	www. majorcitieschiefs. com	801.209.1815 patricia@majorcitieschiefs. com

PRO TIPS FOR PIOS

- Agencies must be proactive in the sharing of essential information to adequately engage with communities in a strategic manner.

- Have a backup PIO to manage the office and social media when you are out of town or need a break.

- Watch other PIOs for the good and bad, and emulate the great things you see.

- Network with fellow spokespersons to create a peer support system.

- Don't be afraid to ask for help when you need it. This is not a sign of weakness. Rather, it demonstrates professionalism.

- Join national communication groups to share best practices and learn from others.

- Conduct site visits by visiting other agencies, especially if you are new to the profession.

- If you are not a sworn officer, ride with your agency's officers to immerse yourself in the police culture. This will pay dividends when you ask to profile officers on social media.

PART II

HOW DO YOU
COMMUNICATE
STRATEGICALLY?

CHAPTER 3

MANAGING TRADITIONAL MEDIA

My former boss, Will D. Johnson, a police chief with an uncanny ability to bridge the gap between news organizations and police bureaucracies, understood the power of traditional media like no one else. He once jokingly told me that a strategic communication advisor/PIO has more power, arguably, than he did as police chief of a major city. "Chris, you have the power to call a press conference and summon every media outlet and reporter in town within a matter of hours," he said.

He was trying to instill in me that a press conference elevates the stature of the topic and situation. With that power comes enormous responsibility. As we assess incidents, we must engage in strategic thinking to determine whether we want to raise the public profile of an incident through a formal press event or attempt to de-escalate by simply releasing a written statement. There are no right answers for most of our agencies' challenges. However, there are many wrong answers. All these decisions come down to strategically approaching the issues to resolve the community's questions.

Growing up as a baby PIO in the Dallas-Fort Worth market, I had the luxury to have several veteran reporters take me under their wings to train me on what works—what gets covered and what goes into file thirteen (trash can, for non-military folks).

Brandon Todd, now an anchor for the KDFW Fox 4, and Fil Alvarado, who retired from the same station, taught me that news stories need a "peg." A news peg is like a hook or the reason for the story. Timeliness, urgency, currency, and newsworthiness are elements of news pegs that increase the likelihood of coverage. Brandon and Fil would remind me why my police academy graduation news release would never be covered. It's simple—every agency has academy graduations. To find a news peg, I would have to tell my story as something different—maybe an academy graduation where a father is retiring the same day that his son is being sworn in. This basic principle of a news peg revolutionized my approach to breaking news for my agency.

I credit learning the ropes on my first critical incident—a major crash and resulting murder of a Good Samaritan—with another journalist, Scott Gordon, now retired from KXAS NBC 5. His sage advice never left me. Speed in responding matters most at the scene of a breaking news incident. Yes, facts are critical, but trying to ensure you have a perfect fact set (which is problematic in policing, especially at the onset of an incident) means you will be too caught up in every aspect of a scene. As a result, you will be too slow in responding.

Why is this bad? Because the media will get their interview from someone else. All too often, someone else won't have any facts but doesn't mind getting their five minutes of fame. I learned from that first day that facts are necessary, responses are more needed, and the media providing our information to the community is needed the most.

WHAT ABOUT THE MEDIA FUNCTION?

Over the years, when we hired new officers, we would meet with the recruits, who would be dressed in fancy suits to impress the command staff on their first day at the police academy. Part of the formality included going around the classroom and asking the recruit officers to stand and tell us a little about their background and what they wanted to do at the department as they embarked on their new careers.

The most common answer would be that they joined the law enforcement profession to help others. They wanted to make a positive difference in the community. Some would express that they wanted to be a detective in homicide, join the department's SWAT team, or fly drones. Regardless of their background or experience, in all the years I have been a part of this ceremonial welcoming exercise, I have never heard anyone say they joined the department to be a public information officer or work with the media.

These police officers are embarking on a journey that will place them in many different situations helping others, suppressing evil, and upholding the tenets of nobility, all of which will generate media and public interest. Yet most new officers rarely think about the role of media in our society. Moreover, I believe our profession does a poor job of educating police officers on how and why we should communicate.

Law enforcement agencies characteristically claim "transparency" in mission and goal statements, but do we always strive for transparency with our communities and the media? As Julie Parker, a crisis communications expert and former director of media relations for two major police agency, put it, "If you publicly describe your organization as transparent, whether you work in communications or not, ask yourself if that's a true statement. If not, encourage leadership to eliminate that description from your messaging." I couldn't agree more that we sometimes talk a good game; however, it takes organizational commitment to fully realize transparency while working with media.

WHAT DO OUR OFFICERS THINK ABOUT MEDIA?

I believe that police officers have an inherent distrust of the media. Take a poll at your agency and see how many people will raise their hands to volunteer to speak with the media. You will be lucky to have anyone express interest. Where does this come from, and why is it ingrained in law enforcement culture? I attribute it to perceptions of broadcast television media and the steady barrage of negative news that society is routinely exposed to.

A law enforcement agency's media and public relations staffing and budget are minuscule compared to patrol operations and investigative units. And rightly so because our main job is protecting the public. Even though a media role may not garner as much, it is an important function. This begs the question, if we believe it's important to work with media, how should we interact with them, and who are they?

WHY WE NEED EACH OTHER

Media has access to your community. No matter how many social media followers an agency has, traditional media has much more reach. As they report on incidents and events, our agencies have the information and can confirm details for reporters. With said confirmation and information, the media can help sway public opinion.

Reporters will lose out to their competition if they don't develop good rapport with law enforcement agencies. At the same time, we can suffer if we don't have good relationships with local media. We must work together, even during adverse stories, based on our distinct and important roles.

TRADITIONAL MEDIA

Defining traditional media will assist us as we move forward. I am setting aside citizen journalists, internet bloggers, and social media users for the time being, as the approach to working with these types of nontraditional "media" can be different compared to legacy news outlets. It would be wise to understand that most traditional news organizations have a digital reach and presence on social media. Some magazines may publish exclusively online.

Reporters typically attend college and obtain a bachelor's degree in journalism or communication. The average salary in 2023 was $57,527 a year.[14] The larger the news market, the higher the earning potential. As an anchor at a major station or in the national networks, the salaries can go up exponentially. This also explains why newspapers usually receive recent journalism graduates even though they try to remain relevant in the digital space. They require you to establish new relationships often and provide education on interacting with your agency.

TRIAL BY FIRE WITH TRADITIONAL MEDIA

For those with the knowledge of the art of strategic communication, you will never appoint someone to a position as a strategic advisor/PIO without providing them with the proper training and immersing them into the organization's culture. But even with this and a good support network, there will always be a little "trial by fire" for newbie PIOs. Learning the ropes and building relationships with traditional media is a natural byproduct. Here's how my story unfolded.

Before 2011, I was working on a uniformed traffic assignment. As a highway drug interdiction sergeant in Arlington, it was nonstop action consisting of car chases, illicit drug seizures, and cartel-linked arrests. Media relations were not even on my radar at the time. Then, the controversy regarding the militarization of policing took storm across the country, and within a few months, our interdiction unit was disbanded and converted to a commercial vehicle enforcement squad. Grant monies dedicated to domestic highway enforcement dried up as priorities at the federal level changed.

I remember the day I was called and informed that I would be reassigned to a new unit. I was out of town on vacation, touring the countryside of Vermont while sampling some of the best maple syrup I had ever had. My chief was on the other end of the phone, and we exchanged pleasantries before getting to the real business. He informed me that when I returned, he needed me to take the reins of the media office. I remember thinking, why in the hell would I want to work with the media? Even though my thoughts were adrift, I responded professionally and thanked the chief for the new job opportunity. Everyone knows that you don't turn down an opportunity from your boss. There was also speculation that serving as a PIO can accelerate your career progression. Little did I know that this new assignment would unequivocally change my life and career trajectory forever—it did indeed progress my career quickly.

The first few weeks were spent learning the new role and what was expected. My first real test came when our mayor was being targeted with death threats by a "not so nice" guy who owned a sexually oriented business in the city. I encountered my first officer misconduct case, which dealt with a veteran officer who allegedly exposed himself to a female motorist during a traffic stop. Furthermore, my first critical incident involved a man who caused a multiple-car pileup and fatality crash, then shot a Good Samaritan who had stopped to help. All these incidents transpired while I was inexperienced, in a role chosen for me by someone else, and with relatively little knowledge of how to interact with the media.

Sometimes, you have to make the best of a situation. Rather than fret over my inability to think strategically and execute well, I decided to look at peers across the country. I had an intense drive to learn more. I remember getting the opportunity to attend the social media SMILE Conference in Vancouver later that year and meeting Seattle Police Sergeant Sean Whitcomb, now retired and working at Sony. He introduced me to the world of the IACP. He said an entire section of PIOs met twice yearly and had conferences in important locations across the US.

I was sold on the idea of joining the IACP. Still, I would have to convince my boss, James Hawthorne, an assistant police chief who later went on to a police chief role at a neighboring school district. Luckily for me, James was the one who had sent me to Vancouver in the first place.

Sean also persuaded me to conduct site visits. In 2012, I visited the Boston Police Department, the Baltimore Police Department, and the New York City Police Department. I also attended my first IACP conference, which resulted in strong peer relationships and networks that later paid dividends for me and my agencies. I hold the many PIOs/communicators who took the time to invest in my professional development in high regard.

Following this example could help alleviate some of the trial-by-fire that the appointed strategic communication advisor/PIO will undoubtedly experience. They will need a professional network that can be relied upon during a crisis.

Send your people to conferences. Allow them to join communicator organizations. Check for regional training opportunities. Commit to funding site visits to agencies that know how to interact with traditional media.

RELATIONAL SIDE OF TRADITIONAL MEDIA

I was given some good advice as I continued learning the new role. Working alongside the traditional media boils down to relationships. I was reminded that there would be good days and bad ones. There would be positive stories that you want to participate in and others that will cause you to shrug your shoulders and look for ways to get out of doing the interview. The quicker I learned this relational aspect of media, the better my outlook would be in this new role. And, as I look back over the past decade, the advice was spot on.

I never had to worry about a story once I realized journalism professionals were just like you and me. They had families, attended our places of worship, went to the same restaurants, and were doing a job—slightly different from ours, but still a job worth doing. The role of the media in our society is important. The vast majority of journalists are not out to make anyone look bad. It is more about the public and the story. Once we as a profession truly grasp that, our media interactions and results will improve.

I desire to get leaders to see the media in a more favorable light. It would be best if you didn't fall into that same trap I initially did, thinking that the media were always out to get us. Sure, there will be stories that we do not want to run. There will be misconduct stories that embarrass our agencies. There will be controversial force incidents that erode public confidence. As with any profession, you may encounter individuals who are not the best to work with. But there will also be opportunities for you to trumpet the great work that your people do daily through the media—based upon relationships.

RELATIONSHIPS MATTER

I took those strong media relationships with me when I moved from Arlington to a new agency. As a result, within a few weeks of my being appointed as police chief, our little agency of fifty-three employees was routinely being profiled in the media. They had never been on the news for much of anything before my arrival. I am not boasting about this—it's just the facts: relationships matter.

In most major markets, professionalism is commonplace in the traditional media. This is a major distinction between dealing with "self-proclaimed" journalists and professional journalists. As a professional journalist, educational requirements, on-the-job training, and a code of ethics are standard. Also, the longer an advisor/PIO is in the role, the better. It takes time and energy to foster relationships.

I cannot tell you how many folks have reached out to me over the years with thanks for the way I treated them. They knew I was fair, and even if I didn't have the answer or was unable to release the details at that very moment, I still responded, and we worked through it. As a police leader or spokesperson, you must make time to build positive relationships. It will be too late to wait until a big incident or event.

ENHANCING SKILLS

As a new leader, one of the first steps for you and your advisor/ PIO is to visit your local news stations. Even if your jurisdiction falls within a news feeder market that does not generate regular community news, drive out of town to see the broad-cast television news station and newspapers that would service your area if something became newsworthy. As part of your advance planning for this field trip, tell the news organization you want to build a positive relationship with and exchange contact information. This olive branch of showing interest will go a long way.

In larger markets, it would be great for leaders and communicators to sit through a morning or afternoon newsroom meeting. This is where the magic happens: reporters pitching story ideas, producers and assignment editors planning follow-ups to stories, assigning out crews and photographers. Throw in some breaking news, and everything gets shuffled real fast.

This will start your relationship journey as well. Similar to police ride-alongs, news organizations typically have an open-door policy allowing people to attend their daily news meetings. I made rounds with all the television stations, radio hubs, and newspapers. It was fascinating to see how a pitched or assigned story becomes news by the end of the day. It was also an opportunity to build a positive relationship with reporters, editors, producers, and staffers in the newsroom. Don't forget about the folks behind the cameras, either. Camera operators can make you look good and will gladly impart their advice and skills to assist you as both a subject and in developing your own content. You can learn everything from white balancing a camera, getting the sound right, shooting creative angles, and utilizing light to make your subject look their best.

One of the advantages of attending these meetings is the opportunity to talk about your media relations philosophy, if you have already developed it, and your desire to make the law enforcement agency accessible to reporters. Snag some business cards or contact information so that your team can build a media distribution list. There is still tremendous value in pushing news releases out to media lists versus solely relying on social media or forcing media to follow all the social platforms to keep up with your agency. They are busy, too, and by taking a few minutes to push a release to them, you are assisting them in making decisions on what to cover.

Host annual media mixers or events. Meet the reporters and staffers in your market to develop positive relationships. Invite your command staff and officers to attend so you can showcase the diversity and talent of your law enforcement team. During the mixer, don't be bashful about soliciting feedback on how you are doing with the media. Constructive feedback can prevent future problems. It also allows traditional media to share better ways to communicate with them.

INTEGRITY AND TRUST

Leaders only have their integrity, and once that bond of trust has been broken, your credibility will be in serious question with the news media and the public. Credibility is all we have, whether in the leader's seat or a spokesperson's role. Integrity doesn't mean that you always know the right answers. Integrity comes down to the facts you present to the community, utilizing traditional media and social media to convey your authenticity and credibility. A good leader acknowledges these points and corrects any misinformation if facts change.

The bottom line is that trust is the most important thing for a leader and public information officer. That means that when a question comes in related to an incident that cannot be immediately answered, rather than misguide the reporter or community, acknowledge that the organization is not ready to speak on that subject. News media will understand that there are facts that sometimes cannot be released. By taking a few moments to explain why you can't release the information right now, you continue to build credibility. Work hard to establish yourself as being accessible and someone who would tell the truth every time, no matter what the topic is.

To build relationships with news media, I gave my personal mobile phone number out, with the caveat that they would not call me in the middle of the night unless it were serious. I never played dumb or alleged that I didn't know something when, in fact, I did. The best lesson for new leaders is not to avoid difficult or controversial stories. By being accessible and responsive, leaders will begin that steady climb of becoming trusted with news media.

WHAT DOES THE MEDIA REALLY WANT?

The TV show *Dragnet* can serve as a reminder that the media wants the facts. In addition to factual statements, they need a sound bite. The media also wants access to incident scenes, our people, and the leader. They want us to be professional. They want video—initially only for television media, but now, even radio and print media desire to embed video on news websites and social media. The media wants to capture emotion. They need verification and confirmation before reporting (or at least that's what we hope for). The media strives to be relevant, meaning stories that affect and matter to communities.

They sometimes ask for opinions, something that typically is determined by leaders. In most stories, we shy away, as we should, from offering opinions. In some stories, an opinion may be relevant if it comes from the organization's leader. Examples may include op-ed pieces or doing a story on gun control.

Oh, and when do they want all this information? Now. Within reason, we should get the information out in a timely manner. Let's delve a bit deeper into a few of these concepts.

ACCESSIBILITY AND RESPONSIVENESS

In addition to maintaining your integrity, it is important to remain accessible and responsive. Many chiefs and sheriffs hide in their offices and refuse to talk with the media. By creating an environment where the policymaker is unavailable, you communicate that the public side of policing is unimportant. Respond to emails. Return phone calls. By being accessible as an agency head and PIO, you are placing your agency ahead of any discomfort you may have. Members of the media are appreciative when they can have access to other team members in the organization as well, including the agency head.

You should not be the sole face of everything that happens, good and bad, within the organization. Leaders sometimes need some high cover, and it may not be beneficial for the agency head to tackle an adverse story where all the facts and proposed remedies are not yet readily apparent. On the same token, it may be extremely important for the agency head to be out in front of major incidents to convey a position of strength and unity in resolving the crisis at hand.

NO COMMENT

I'll keep this section simple with a quote from my good friend and mentor John Miller, who previously worked with the New York City Police Department and was a regular contributor for CNN: "No comment ever stopped a story." If we understand what John was saying, it means that "no comment" is a comment and will be reported as such.

APPROACHABILITY

It may be stating the obvious, but no one likes a bully or someone who is not approachable. Be kind and patient with the media. Assume that there will always be many new faces in the news profession, and not all of them will have the same training and expertise as their predecessors.

PLAIN SPEAK

As a new spokesperson, one of the first tasks was learning how to communicate effectively. Reporters took me under their wings and showed me the ropes. I learned how to avoid police jargon and acronyms. Leaders and communicators do not want to sound like bureaucratic press releases. It became a simple one-on-one conversation between the reporter and me without regard for the microphone, camera, and lights. This premise also applies to multiple reporters simultaneously: always have a candid and genuine conversation. And I quickly learned that wearing mirrored sunglasses during an outside interview is not cool unless you are Tom Cruise.

It may be surprising to learn this: the average reading level in the US is equivalent to the seventh or eighth grade, according to the U.S. Literacy Project Foundation.[15] Readability can relate to message penetration and how your audience consumes the information you are saying or writing. Online reading can be different also. Many studies have shown that people scan web posts and only read about 18 percent of what's included on the page.[16]

Imagine what happens when you prepare a long post with several paragraphs for Facebook. Coupled with people's short attention spans, don't be discouraged to learn that most people liking or commenting are originally drawn to the post by the photo or graphic. After the thumbs-up click, many continue scrolling. This is one of the reasons that traditional media create headlines or attention grabbers to draw an audience into the article or post.

BAD NEWS

Remember that bad news has a limited shelf life. Your agency will not be stuck in a bad news quagmire forever. You will learn strategies to mitigate bad news. As danger is inherent in law enforcement, so is bad news. It will happen. You will get through it.

ICING A STATION

Icing is when the agency removes a news station from receiving news releases and advisories. Some agencies even go a step further and refuse to do interviews with a particular station. The premise behind icing is that you are "teaching them a lesson" for some egregious thing the station allegedly did to your agency. In theory, I understand why some leaders may desire to engage in this behavior. In reality, I have not seen much benefit; quite the contrary, I have seen agencies royally torched by a news station during icing. It's a much better tactic to sit down with the news station and talk through the challenges and differences versus icing them over, even for a short period of time.

MEDIA MARKETS

As a leader and advisor, you must understand your local media market. In Dallas-Fort Worth, we sit in the fifth largest market. On average, media market order starts with New York, Los Angeles, Chicago, Philadelphia, Dallas-Fort Worth, Atlanta, Houston, Washington, DC, Boston, and San Francisco-Oakland-San Jose.[17]

By knowing your markets, you will understand why some local stories may end up in the national airwaves. Many stories originate from feeder markets to the larger newsrooms, so even if you operate in "small town USA," there are chances that stories affecting your community could grow legs and expand across larger swaths of the country.

Media markets also help explain the competitive side of journalism. Make no bones about it—news stations compete with each other. This has to do with advertising dollars. There is a drive to be first and break stories before their competition. How does this affect us? It means the speed at which information flows from law enforcement to media has increased.

With media markets also come newsroom changes. Many markets experience lots of movement. As soon as you develop a great relationship, a reporter moves on. This is to be expected and can be managed. A well-written media guidebook that explains your agency's media philosophy and protocols can help educate new reporters and producers.

HOW DO NEWS STATIONS MAKE MONEY?

News stations sell advertising space to businesses and corporations through commercials. The larger their viewership and audience, the more money they can make.

How do they know who watches what program and how

often? A company called Nielsen measures what content people watch and listen to and conducts cross-market analyses to understand how audiences watch TV and listen to music and podcasts.

WHAT IS NEWS?

News is the same thing happening today that happened yesterday, only to different people. Let that sink in. At its core, every newscast contains various elements that exist daily. There will be shootings, crashes, police incidents, government fraud, and other stories that are deemed relevant.

In our world, the news is often something the agency's leader or their people did, for better or worse, that has now been placed in front of the public and the leader's bosses.

WHAT MAKES NEWS?

Currency allows a story to become news because many people talk about it. This is why the not-so-nice Facebook post that someone creates about your agency and goes viral may generate a news inquiry. News value is determined when a story has one or more elements of news: impact on community or humanity, regionalization (local ties to region), timeliness of information, prominence of the incident (how big a deal is it), conflict, controversy, human interest, doom and gloom (bad weather and storms), feel-good elements and compassion, and novelty or oddity. The more news pegs you can tie to these elements, the better chances that your story will be covered.

There's also a saying in newsrooms that I have found truer than any news value concept: the odd, unusual, and extraordinary make the news.

TEN TYPICAL NEWS VALUES

1. Impact	6. Controversy
2. Regionalization	7. Human interest
3. Timeliness	8. Doom and gloom
4. Prominence	9. Feel-good compassion
5. Conflict	10. Novelty or oddity

Remember that a few things move a potential story idea from Main Street, USA, to a news broadcast. Citizens will call news desks to report a dozen police cars on a street, resulting in a news inquiry. Media monitoring law enforcement radios find story ideas. News organizations have social media monitoring systems with keyword alerts—shooting, bomb, car chase, shots fired, officer down, and other newsworthy terms. Journalists develop close contacts with police officers, creating "sources" who can tip them off when an incident occurs. News releases and media advisories can lead to stories. Prepping a reporter and contacting producers can lead to a story. Social media posts may generate a news story.

TYPICAL NEWSROOM

The news director is kind of like a police chief. You probably won't have much contact with them unless a relationship between your agency and the local station has soured. Assignment editors are considered the gatekeepers of the newsroom. Get to know them personally. Reporters are the face of the newsroom. Multimedia journalists respond to scenes, offer accounts on camera, and can film and edit their own stories. Producers are usually in charge of writing and executing the show. Stringers cover breaking news and smaller events. Freelancers may work on assignment for a station or operate like a stringer, gathering information and visuals from scenes and selling their stories to newsrooms.

A decade ago, there was a clear delineation among beat reporters, general assignment reporters, consumer news, and investigative reporters. While some markets may still have clearly defined roles, I have recently seen a crossover among reporters and news officials, likely due to budgetary considerations. Regardless of how your local newsroom operates, get back to the basics of relationships with all the job functions. This will bode well for your department regarding covering stories and responding to breaking news incidents.

NEWS RELEASES

According to some seasoned professionals, the almighty news release, an ancient relic, can still be used to communicate an agency's position formally. News releases can also be used to announce new programs, highlight cases that most news stations would be interested in, or close out a critical incident. News releases can serve as a historical wrap-up communication and be one of the agency's final processes, certainly after the spokesperson has "provided sound" (spoken to the media).

A news release should contain a few basic elements. A professional letterhead and contact information should be included along with the following components:

- Date and time of release
- Title describing the release (Think of something that will grab the news desk to want to read your release. Remember, news desks get hundreds if not thousands of emails daily)
- Introductory statement (brief)
- Body of the release—contains a logical sequence and explanation of the event, incident, or item being described
- Obtain approval before distribution. Read, reread, and have another person do a final proof

- Consider attachments to supplement the news release (booking photos, affidavits, visuals, and video links)

Avoid police jargon and acronyms and use "plain speak," as discussed earlier. Start with the date and time of the response or incident, along with the location and type of call. This can be accomplished using the five *w*'s—who, what, when, where, and why. The first four are self-explanatory. The "why" can sometimes be ascertained; however, it is often unknown. Incorporate paragraphs to convey a particular idea within a group of sentences. When the thought or idea changes, start a new paragraph.

Strive for consistent, clear meaning, accurate statements, and brevity in news releases. Chronological order works well. Quotes may be added to expound on the topic and provide perspective from a leader. Try to write in the third person, if possible.

NEWS MEDIA LIST

News releases need to be disseminated on time. Start accumulating an email and phone list of reporters and news stations. Add their emails to your list as new contacts emerge from email inquiries. This official news media list needs to be accessible from off-premises as well, so plan accordingly and have a spreadsheet set up to aid in quickly disseminating releases to news outlets and reporters. New communicators and leaders can ask neighboring agencies to borrow their list as they start.

Don't forget to include elected officials, as approved by your boss, and other important community stakeholders. A good rule of thumb used in North Texas is including other PIOs to broaden their awareness. Employees should also receive the news release.

If disseminating via email, always blind copy to prevent someone from replying to all or disclosing your list inadvertently. Once the news release has been sent, publish the release on your website in a set location and on your social media feeds, if appropriate.

MASTER CONTACT LIST

Create and maintain a master contact list of important organizations and people. Sometimes, a news release may need to be pushed to people not in a news media role. For example, if my agency is releasing something about a school incident, it would behoove me to forward the release to their superintendent, head law enforcement agent, and communications personnel. In addition, depending on your jurisdictional boundaries, you may include neighboring agencies for awareness.

MEDIA ADVISORIES

Media advisories are typically used to announce an event, traffic closure (not due to a crash), photo opportunities, media mixers, academy graduations, and programs. They follow a similar template as a news release but are more concise.

AGENCY-WRITTEN STATEMENTS

Not to be confused with formal news releases or advisories, a written statement is a technique to respond to an inquiry about an incident in writing. There may be some strategy in releasing a written statement in cases where the agency decides not to go on camera for an interview or does not want to elevate the issue through a formal news release.

An apt use of an agency-written statement could be when the organization is notified about a use of force that occurred but has not had time to conduct the appropriate review. In the interest of calming community concerns, a written statement might read, "The Anytown Police Department is aware of a video circulating on social media purporting to show an encounter between one of our officers and a community member. The department is looking into this matter and will share more information as it becomes available."

FACTORS INCLUDED IN A WRITTEN STATEMENT (ADVERSE INCIDENT)

There are many ways to prepare a written statement. One way is following the COPS acronym. It was developed to hit four major high points when dealing with situations requiring empathy and conveying that the agency is aware of and dealing with the incident. This method creates a buffer between community outcries and the agency for a short time until additional communication efforts are published and released.

- **C**ompassion –As an agency, you want to show genuine compassion and concern for the situation.

- **O**wnership—People need to know that you are aware of the situation and have the ability and capacity to deal with it. This reinforces confidence that your organization can manage the incident.

- **P**oint-of-View—This is the information your agency needs the community to know. You are conveying relevant information, known at the time, to keep things in a box.

- **S**hare—The last step is to share the statement, written or verbal, with the appropriate audience. This can be accomplished through an emailed statement to media, a social media post, or a video.

MESSAGING CUBE

The messaging cube was developed for certain types of interviews or press conferences that you may be faced with. This is an additional initial tool as you plan how to deal with a situation or incident.

- **A**uthority—Start by explaining the reason law enforcement is involved in the first place. Authority for police intervention comes from many different sources.

- **B**alance—What you release should balance what the community needs to know and what needs to be kept confidential to protect the ongoing investigation. Spokespersons and leaders must also balance what is legally releasable and what is not.

- **C**all to action—Give your audience something to do. Do you need them to check their surveillance cameras? Do they need to go to a church to pick their kids up? Do you need tips to aid in the investigation? Do they simply need awareness of this incident?

- **D**evotion—Show your enthusiasm and thank others—patrol officers, investigators, dispatchers, individual persons, partner agencies, firefighters, community, Good Samaritans, and media, as appropriate. Devotion to the duty of serving, protecting, and the rule of law can also be a good closer.

Many variations of the messaging cube can also be found online or at communicator conferences. For example, Ken White and Gail Pennybacker developed the Message Bases strategy for the Federal Bureau of Investigation in 2013.[18] Regardless of what system you incorporate, the premise remains the same.[19]

INTERVIEWS

Interviews with individual reporters occur frequently. Once you ascertain the FACTS and approach the topic with the messaging cube, it's easy to converse with the reporter. In some cases, an interview may involve multiple stations simultaneously.

As you prepare for the interview, strive for a relaxed yet professional appearance. It's OK to ask the reporter what questions they may have before the interview starts. If the interview is not live, you can ask for a redo if you make a mistake.

Practice with a coworker before the interview. Have your colleague ask you questions. Try to anticipate questions that may arise.

Always check your appearance before getting in front of a camera. Silence notifications on your devices before conducting the interview. Be aware of your surroundings and background before setting up the interview.

EXCLUSIVES

An exclusive means that you only do this interview with a particular outlet. Giving an exclusive on a topic likely to have additional media interest will only frustrate other news outlets and could strain relationships. Over my tenure, I have only participated in a handful of exclusives, and they typically dealt with situations where a reporter was doing a lot of deep background on an issue; therefore, the bulk of the leg-work was media-initiated.

Be careful handling exclusives with individual reporters, especially as a leader. If one station continues to get exclusives over other stations, it will appear as if the agency is biased. Nothing good will come from this type of appearance.

EMBARGOES

In limited situations, media may want to prefilm a speaker, knowing they will run the piece later at the appropriate time. An example would be when the leader is about to present the department's annual report to their elected body and review crime rates. A news station may have interest in covering that type of story, especially if crime rates have spiraled upward, so the best approach may be to sit down for the interview with an agreement to embargo the story until after the presentation.

MEDIA TERMS WORTH KNOWING

You may hear terms like "on the record," "off the record," or "on background." There are many media jargon terms, and it's best to ask for clarification to fully understand them before commenting since other people can interpret these terms differently. On the record is straightforward and means that statements made can be officially attributed to the person with the authority to make the statements and agency. On-the-record statements are the bulk of what a leader and communicator will provide reporters and news media.

Off the record typically means that shared information cannot be used for publication or attributed to the person sharing the information. While "off the record" sounds easy enough, it can spell major trouble for the agency if something is reported without being properly sourced. I can count on one hand how many times I ever went off the record, and it was always with reporters with whom I had developed deep and trustworthy relationships. One example of going off the record was an instance involving a line-of-duty death involving sensitive information that the agency was not going to release; however, a reporter received unauthorized information through a confidential source. In that case, going off the record prevented the leaked information from running while preserving the relationship with the reporter.

On background typically means that the statements and information can be used, but only under conditions agreed upon with the source providing information. Background can also be used to assist a reporter with understanding a police tactic, as an example, to give context to the news story. There are media schools and books where one can learn further terminology of news organizations.

PRESS CONFERENCES

Press conferences elevate a situation compared to individual interviews. Agencies usually reserve press conferences for something major. Examples may include an update on an officer-involved shooting, a major new program or initiative, an employee misconduct resolution, or a new partnership with comments from other law enforcement agencies.

When the agency hosts a press conference, most traditional media will attend. Considerations include who will speak, the role of multiple speakers, if necessary, what the background will look like, and the style of decorum.

Specialized equipment may be needed, such as a mult-box, which allows multiple news stations to plug into and have only one microphone at the podium. No one wants to have twelve different mics attached to a podium.

If flags are present, ensure they are displayed properly. There is nothing worse than receiving a stern email from a proud military veteran that the US flag was not correct. By having all of the background and imaging elements in proper order, your agency is telegraphing that they are professional.

Plan an exit strategy, especially during controversial incidents. Your exit needs to appear graceful. Gone are the days when reporters should be shouting questions as a police chief scurries off stage. It's also a good rule of thumb to have a trusted advisor stand in the back of the room, within view, and raise their hand when the press conference should wrap up. This visual cue will allow the speaker to announce that there is only time for a few more questions and signal an impending end to the conference.

Also, don't set artificial future timelines for additional interviews. The next update should come out when you have something of value to provide.

HOW MANY SPEAKERS?

This should be approached strategically. Each situation should dictate who speaks and how many speak. It's possible that the strategic communications advisor/PIO opens the press event up and then turns it over to the agency head. I have also seen huge press conferences where multiple chiefs, sheriffs, and even politicians have a speaking role. Every speaker should have their defined role and sequencing. This will also need to be choreographed for questions.

SHOULD I TAKE QUESTIONS?

Absolutely. Always allow some time for questions. On questions where you do not know the answer or cannot divulge the information, acknowledge that you will find out, or it would be premature to release those facts. Answer truthfully.

NON-ENGLISH-SPEAKING AUDIENCES

Agencies should know their target audiences and plan to have interpreters to address diverse populations. For example, I try to have a Spanish speaker available to provide sound to local media during interviews and press conferences. Depending on your intended audience, having staff who are bilingual can maximize communication reach to diverse communities, which is vital in fighting crime and building trust.

AMERICAN SIGN LANGUAGE (ASL) INTERPRETER

The Americans with Disabilities Act of 1990 establishes guidelines for the communication needs of hard of hearing and deaf persons. While not required in most law enforcement briefings, it is something that leaders and advisors should consider during press conferences when pertinent information will be shared. Utilizing an ASL interpreter conveys to this audience that the department cares enough to address communication barriers.

INVESTIGATIVE PIECES

There are times when an investigative reporter may come knocking on your door. In my experience, agencies will usually know when something may be pending because there may be little hints. For example, agencies may start to see several open records requests and FOIA inquiries surrounding a particular topic area in the department. Chances are that a producer for the investigative news team is getting their homework done before they reach out. There is nothing to fret about once you are approached. Gone are the days when a sensational reporter chases a police executive down with a camera and microphone, demanding an answer. Most of the time, agencies will have ample notice as investigative stories are usually in-depth and require much lead time on the news station's end.

Deciding whether an agency should participate on camera includes weighing the pros and cons. While many of these stories can feel like they are out to get you, I can recall several investigative pieces where the police department came out on top.

If an agency agrees to an interview, the look and feel of the interview environment will be much different compared to a normal interview. Investigative photographers often like to bring dramatic lights and set the mood for the story. The interview will typically have a good vibe before starting and immediately turn to business once the questions begin. Maintain your composure and communicate professionally with the reporter. If you must stand your ground on a topic, do exactly that. There is nothing wrong with standing on facts and reiterating your position if the reporter continues to press in a certain direction.

TO RECORD OR NOT RECORD

Another possibility is to consider setting up your own camera. While this may not be perceived favorably by the reporter if they are doing a "gotcha" hit piece, it may be worth having a copy of the interview should you decide later to present your full responses to the community. Again, this is totally up to you, and I rarely had to resort to that tactic. When you think about the relationship with local media, it includes relationships with investigative reporters. They want to get the story right while balancing fairness between the issue being analyzed and the agency's response.

Like investigative pieces, there are times when you will decide to go on camera during controversial, difficult, or adversarial interviews or press conferences. Sometimes, I made my recording to place the unedited version on our social media. I have also completed far more interviews and conferences that I did not record. You will have to make this decision, and there are varying opinions. I would say that if you are recording solely to send a message to the news reporter, then I would shy away from that style of tactic. If there is a legitimate reason to record the interview so that it can be distributed to your community, then by all means, proceed.

WHAT ABOUT RADIO?

Radio is alive and well in America. These are some of the easiest interviews to do. Most of the time, the reporter will have you telephone and talk on a recorded line. Make sure you know whether this is a live segment or prerecorded.

SPEAKING OF LIVE—ANY ADVICE?

One of the lessons I learned the hard way was in 2012 at a murder-suicide scene. Investigators and the incident commander had briefed me. I crafted my messaging utilizing the FACTS and messaging cube methods. I approached the bank of cameras and asked if everyone was ready. There were some mumbles about still needing a white balance and audio check.

As I was standing there waiting, I did not realize that some stations, which were already ready, had begun broadcasting live to their audiences. As the uncomfortable silence continued, one reporter made a joke, and I responded to the joke—live on television! Needless to say, I learned a valuable lesson that day. When you walk into a live situation, start when you get into position. The other stations can catch up.

WHEN TO DO INTERVIEWS AND PRESS CONFERENCES

You should always ask yourself if you should go on camera. Don't hesitate to ask the news desk and reporter about the story's direction. Will the community be better served by you going on camera? How will the department appear on camera compared to releasing a written statement or advising of facts in an email or telephone call?

There are advantages to going on camera, even if the news story might be adverse. Getting in front of a story may have some strategic value. Most of the time, your agency will be asked for an interview during an evolving incident. Information can be readily shared with media using the FACTS and messaging cube.

Regular interview media briefings should be considered when an incident is ongoing, such as a barricaded person. There is no exact science on how often to schedule recurring briefings; however, do not schedule the next briefing unless you have new information that can be shared. Nothing is more embarrassing than calling a news briefing with no refreshed content—this will invariably lead to a litany of questions.

One thing to remember when deciding whether to hold an interview briefing is that someone else might be if you're not talking. In other words, the media will find ways to fill the void of silence.

BACKDROPS

When you decide to provide an interview at your shop, dedicate a space that can accommodate media. Preferably, invest in a backdrop—anything from a step-and-repeat banner displaying your logos to a mural that contains your branding symbols, images, or photos. Outdoors in front of your station might provide a good visual appeal to enhance a story.

In the field, you can use marked patrol units or other areas that will not detract from the incident as background. Be mindful of your surroundings; while media loves visuals in the background to reinforce the topic, we must be respectful at incident scenes.

Similarly, do you want people to stand behind the speaker(s) when hosting a press conference? Some departments routinely post command staff behind the podium and speaker. Others stick to a one-person-at-a-time approach. There is no right or wrong way. Just ensure the people in the background are not fidgeting with their phones, picking their noses, or making unpleasant facial expressions or grimaces. Trust me, those looks come off tacky and occur often.

PODIUM

Podiums are cheap. You need one that is portable. Also, ensure enough space on the front to attach a patch or badge logo. Podiums add a professional look when conducting certain types of interviews, especially during press conferences when a speaker may need to access notes.

LIGHTS

You need lights so the speaker will look their best. Lume Cube produces some of the best lights on the market cheaply. Their studio panel lighting kit works great and is portable, so they can also be used in the field.

MEDIA STAGING AREAS

A media staging area is useful at scenes. Evolving and dynamic scenes may require staging reporters further from the incident scene. A static scene may afford a closer location. It's a good idea to advise the media as quickly as possible before they set up. Many times, a first-line supervisor may set the media staging area up. I have found that emailing the news desk with the location is best. Don't throw the location out on social media; you would communicate to the general public that something big is going on—and invite just about anyone inquisitive enough to show up at the scene.

Here are a few tips to consider:

- Wherever the public can go, the media can go.
- If you don't want media in a certain area, mark it off with crime scene tape.

- Don't stick the media two blocks from a stabilized incident scene. Remember, part of their job is to get visuals. Being close to a stabilized scene doesn't hinder operations.

- In my experience, the media (at least in the US) does not air dead bodies that are not covered. Setting a staging area with that awareness is helpful regarding scene placement.

- During crises or critical incidents that generate significant public interest, media may turn to "team coverage," which means that one reporter or photographer may stay in the staging area while another reporter walks the perimeter of the incident to gather visuals or interviews.

- Change the staging area location if a hostile crowd develops, which may interfere with your interview ability.

- At scenes with heightened levels of controversy, assign an overwatch officer to keep the speaker safe during the interview.

MEDIA AIRCRAFT

Helicopters, especially in larger markets, may arrive on the scene of breaking news. If the rotor noise or live feeds interfere with a police operation, contact the news desk. In my experience, the media is responsive to requests to insert delays on their live feeds or move away from an incident so as not to interfere with officer safety. In cases where they don't move away, request a temporary flight restriction through the Federal Aviation Administration until the incident is resolved.

MEDIA TRAINING FOR EMPLOYEES

Every employee should be trained in your media relations philosophy and policy. This is also a great way to get their active participation in submitting favorable story ideas. Training should also include how to treat reporters at scenes, what information is releasable and what is not, how to set up media staging areas, and how to be aware of camera angles.

Early in my career, I remember getting a call from my boss, who was furious about a news video on television. The media was reporting on a fatal crash, and he said that two of our officers were standing in the middle of the interstate highway with the wrecked car in the background and appeared to be laughing. As I attempted to calm him and explain that the officers were likely telling stories that had nothing to do with the fatal crash, I realized we had failed the agency by not making employees aware of issues like these.

NEWS CYCLES

A news cycle can be defined as the time that passes between news programs. Many factors, including breaking news, can affect what is covered during a news cycle. As police officers, we rarely think about news cycles and how they can affect our organization for better or worse. Think of leveraging the power of the news cycle to your advantage. A well-planned news release announcing a great new initiative could gain positive traction when disseminated during a favorable news cycle.

It could be said that there is no daily news cycle in modern times. It's continuous. It's like a treadmill. The main takeaway for leaders is to have positive police-related content deemed newsworthy and get negative stories out of the news cycle as quickly as possible.

As we discuss news cycles, the conversation will be divided between bad news and positive press. It should be no surprise that leaders should carefully consider what time and what day of the week to release notable items. If you are staring down some adverse news, Mondays, Tuesdays, Wednesdays, and Thursdays are typically not good days to send a news release out. There is a reason why the White House pushes out a five o'clock Friday news dump. Viewership and ratings fall off as people enter the weekend.

Here are a few ways to remember the news cycles when dealing with negative press:

- Miserable Mondays—Try not to release anything adverse.

- Terrible Tuesdays—Again, don't release anything adverse, if possible.

- Waiting Wednesdays—Keep on holding your release with negative news.

- Tricky Thursdays—You could possibly release on a Thursday, say at 5 p.m., but it can be tricky. When in doubt, wait until Friday.

- Favorable Fridays—This is your day of the week to release adverse news.

Let's consider news cycles from the opposite perspective, when we have something great to release that we desire the whole world to know:

- Magical Mondays—By far, the best day of the week when you have something great to say.

- Terrific Tuesdays—The second best day of the week for good news.

- Winning Wednesdays—Again, Wednesdays will get you in front of the masses.

- Tried and True Thursdays—Thursdays have a strong market viewership for positive press.

- Favorable Fridays—Wait, this is the same for adverse news. While Fridays are OK to use, you won't reach as many people due to declining viewership.

Another consideration for leaders and strategic advisors/PIOs is coordinating the release of adverse news with other agencies. Let's face it: sometimes, you cannot wait until Friday for an adverse story. Maybe a critical incident involving a force encounter happened on a Monday, and public scrutiny is mounting on a Tuesday. There may be some strategic value to contacting your peer agency heads and seeing if they have also been sitting on some adverse news. Experience has demonstrated that there may be less of a blow to your agency if multiple agencies coordinate releasing adverse information at the same time. Before you think this is always the best solution, I would caution that news organizations are wise and may see through these attempts. It comes down to the type of news market you are in and whether other agencies' news releases have relevant value that will minimize the impact of your release.

PITCHING STORIES

With time and experience, you will develop your own methods for pitching stories. Your pitches should align with your strategic communication plan. Giving media video and access to officers and deputies will greatly enhance their willingness to do a story versus a talking head (interview with just the PIO or leader).

Some times are not conducive to pitches. A busy news day will make it harder to land a primetime spot in the newscast. Good relationships with assignment desks can help to get advice on a good day for news.

Don't neglect the possibility that enough visuals, coupled with the story elements, may be enough to get a news station to put a story together without the need to send a reporter. In the blueprint section of this chapter, there is a resource called "Perfect Pitch" to guide your agency in increasing your chances for positive news.

KEYS TO POSITIVE NEWS COVERAGE

The most common question asked is how to get positive news coverage. Unfortunately, there is no secret. Factors mostly beyond your control often affect your ability to obtain coverage. In my experience, it comes down to relationships, story type, and news value.

I will reiterate the importance of forming positive relationships with the news desks, reporters, photographers, anchors, and producers. It takes time to build positive rapport with news media, especially in markets that experience a lot of staff movement. Take the time to understand their code of ethics and their societal role.

Leaders must understand that while favorable news should be an underlying goal, news stations also expect leaders to partner during adverse news situations. Don't fall into the trap of seeking only positive news because all agencies experience missteps, force encounters, misconduct, and violent crimes.

One key concept often overlooked is following up with news outlets once a news release has been disseminated. It doesn't hurt your agency to call the news desks and producers when you want something covered. Remember, these folks may get hundreds of emails and releases a day. During your phone contact, emphasize what you can to separate yourself from your neighboring agencies and other news items in the news cycle. It also doesn't hurt to release a "prerelease" for an event in advance and resend the news release the morning of the event.

Leaders and strategic advisors must be savvy and know when to solicit positive news coverage. Many times in my career, I had the perfect news release ready to send, only to have to delay it due to major breaking news in the market. That's what we refer to as preemptions. Your perfect story gets preempted based upon something else that happened that has greater news value and currency. Rather than get frustrated and squander the news release, wait for the right moment in the news cycle. If you push forward anyway, your story will likely be passed over.

Another important tip for executives is to have something great to discuss. Remember, the odd, unusual, and extraordinary make the news. If you have a story idea containing those elements, the probability that the media will cover the agency is good.

Here is a recent example. Our police department tried to stop the driver of a stolen car, who fled from officers. The suspect jumped out and tried to evade on foot. Two police officers chased after the bad guy during the Texas summer when temperatures were soaring. One of the officers became a little winded and was offered a ride by a Good Samaritan, which he accepted. While the first officer, who remained in the foot chase, was apprehending the suspect in a driveway, the second officer arrived in the "taxi" service by the good-willed neighbor. Oh, and by the way, the first officer has one arm. Now, with all those elements, the odd, unusual, and extraordinary were exceedingly met—stolen car, Good Samaritan helping police, physical limitation not interfering with job, and officers working in the Texas heat to catch the suspect on a serious offense. Within an hour of releasing relevant body camera and dashcam footage, the story was well on its way to becoming an international news story. (Readers will easily find this example through a simple internet search.)

Using video to your advantage can also increase the likelihood that news media will pick up a story. People are drawn to visual stories. While each state has varying laws on releasing videos and dispatching radio audio, there are usually some workarounds to get your story out.

News desks love these approaches. In many cases, they don't even have to assign a reporter. Your footage can run, with accompanying details—provided by you—in a voice-over by the news anchor.

Working with traditional media can be rewarding and has numerous opportunities to showcase our agencies. They have the reach and can inform and educate at the same time. Strive for positive press, and your hard work will pay off.

NEWS RELEASE NOTIFICATIONS

Ah, the part that causes the most stress for leaders. How you notify your boss (or bosses) will depend on their expectations and demands. I will share what has worked well for me. In Arlington, as the chief of staff, I would send a copy of the news release to the police chief before it was sent to the media or community.

Depending on the topic, we would also send a copy to employees about a half hour or so before it became public. Why? Because this builds trust with employees and projects that we care that they get the news first. I have never met an officer who thought it was cool to see the police chief talking about an officer-involved shooting on the news without being aware of said incident.

Don't neglect your city manager, city council, county commissioners, or other "very important people" either. It may be appropriate to include a conversation with civil rights groups, such as the NAACP, LULAC, Asian Americans Advancing Justice, or other social service organizations, especially if the news story will be controversial or affect minority communities.

EMPLOYEE NAMES, PHOTOS, AND OPEN INVESTIGATIONS

Each state has its own public release laws. Follow the guidance in your local jurisdiction. Here are a few things to consider as you determine how your agency will manage requests to identify employees, release photos, and discuss facts concerning an open or pending investigation.

First, develop a policy so that employees know what to expect. Most agencies take an entry photo upon hire. I like to take two photos—one with the standard military pose (nonsmiling) and one with smiling. This gives me options should a request come in. When the media asks for a photo, unless they are filing a formal open records request or FOIA request, you can ask them what the photo will be used for. In many cases during my career, even if the media asked for an employee photo, I could reach out and discuss with the reporter or news desk and get them to move off the topic, as long as the incident was not controversial. A simple conversation and productive relationship go a long way in this topic.

Second, employee names and photos are generally releasable in most states, with one exception. Officers who work in a covert capacity may be subject to certain rules to prevent the disclosure of their identity. Brush up on the laws in your area related to when this protection applies.

Third, many states allow agencies to withhold certain types of information related to open and pending investigations. These could be internal investigations regarding an employee or a criminal investigation in the community. Again, it will depend on what laws apply in your state. For example, Texas generally requires the "basic front sheet" of an offense report to be released upon request, which contains some base-level information.

Finally, above all else, notify affected employees if and when their name, photo, or information is released. That's the right thing to do. Never assume someone else has completed this task. As a leader and advisor, double-check to prevent blowback from an upset employee.

MEDIA MONITORING

Agencies need a way to monitor traditional media and stay in touch with things being said about their departments. There are commercial-based pay solutions where police departments can set up keywords to search across media markets nationwide. An example of a paid service would be TVEyes. There are also free options, which are often less intuitive and may provide fewer alerts, that agencies with limited resources may consider. An example would be setting up Google alerts for certain keywords. Another free option is to have someone manually search the various news outlets for the agency's name and leaders.

The benefit of establishing a monitoring plan is twofold. First, it is important to know what is happening with your agency. This allows the department to correct misinformation, if it exists, on a news story. Second, it will enable new leaders and communicators to learn how the media works. For example, a spokesperson may have provided a two-minute interview; however, the reporter and station cut it down to a few seconds of a sound bite. Monitoring stories one has participated in allows a newly appointed spokesperson to hone their interview skill set and focus on key messages during an interview.

CATALOGING

Similar to monitoring, there is value in cataloging news stories in digital and video form. Our agency downloads relevant news mentions, posts them to our YouTube channel under the category "News Media," and positions them on the website under "Newsroom." This enables community members to access news programming generated from traditional news sources. It also puts the agency in a position to storyboard media exposure over the past year.

BLUEPRINT—CHAPTER 3

TWENTY-SIX TIPS FOR BEFORE, DURING, AND AFTER AN INTERVIEW

1. Do you need to do one? If so, who is the right person to do it? (Consider detectives, officers, dispatchers, and professional staff team members depending on the situation and to showcase the talent and diversity of the agency).

2. Put your boss out there sometimes, strategically, so the community knows who is in charge.

3. Insulate the leader sometimes, which means the advisor/PIO may be on the hook depending on the topic.

4. Consider the advantages or disadvantages of uniform versus business casual clothing, if applicable.

5. Is more than one station asking for an interview? If so, maybe coordinate requests to do them simultaneously.

6. Will the interview be recorded or broadcast live? What about live streaming on social media? It's OK to ask for a "do-over" (if not live).

7. Where will the interview take place? At a scene? At the department? What are the backgrounds available to you to reflect professionalism? If at a scene, take charge to ensure backgrounds are appropriate.

8. It's OK to ask the reporter about the story's direction if needed.

9. Prepare! Get the FACTS and review the messaging cube. Make some notes if needed, but don't read them like a script unless the topic is a high-stakes matter requiring a scripted speech.

10. Check your appearance before the interview (hair, teeth, clothing, uniform). Don't wear sunglasses. Don't chew gum or tobacco (yes, I've seen this during police interviews).

11. Avoid distractions (pens, smartphones, smartwatches, ringers).

12. Always anticipate questions, including surprise ones. Depending on the incident, have someone do some intel gathering about what citizens are telling the media, which may assist you in knowing the direction of questions.

13. Run a mock interview with a peer before stepping up to the camera.

14. When you walk up, assume the camera is recording and the mics are hot.

15. State your name and title so they can check your audio levels. They may also ask you to hold a white card or paper to adjust the camera's color. You might remind everyone to silence their phones.

16. Set the ground rules, identify yourself, and provide a brief opening statement if appropriate.

17. Maintain eye contact with the reporter versus looking into the camera lens. If there are multiple reporters, move your head side to side naturally to appear that you are addressing all stations.

18. Artificial lighting can be overwhelming, especially at night outdoors, so find some focal points to zero in on.

19. Remember to incorporate your key messages and sound bite.

20. Keep sentences and answers concise. Come back to key points as needed.

21. Correct yourself if you say something in error.

22. You can bridge difficult questions by reverting to your key points and sound bite ("While it would be premature to speculate at this point of the investigation, what I can tell you is….").

23. Remain outwardly calm and in control. Don't get mad at difficult questions. Watch your facial expressions and nonverbal cues.

24. Acknowledge if you don't know the answer or cannot say. Remember, "no comment" is a comment.

25. Have an ending strategy and a graceful exit strategy. You can remind reporters that you will work on obtaining any unknown information that is publicly releasable and get back to them.

26. Watch the interview and critique yourself. You can also ask the reporter and media for feedback.

TWENTY-EIGHT TIPS FOR BEFORE, DURING, AND AFTER A PRESS CONFERENCE

1. Press conferences elevate a situation. Decide if it's necessary.

2. Determine who will talk, who will stand with the speaker(s), and who will stand behind the speaker(s). The leader is typically one of the main speakers. A strategic communication advisor may introduce the leader and other speakers.

3. If people will stand beside or behind the speaker(s), ensure they have a good appearance and remain professional. I personally do not like the "let's have twelve people standing behind the speaker" approach, but this is your call.

4. If more than one person will be speaking, determine the appropriate order. Create a press conference agenda to keep everything on task. As you consider who should speak, remember that people have egos, and asking one person and not another could create hurt feelings or strain a professional relationship.

5. Invite *all* the media (no one should be left out). Make sure your announcement provides ample time for the media to organize and plan for the press conference.

6. Prepare the press conference location. Make sure flags or other visuals are displayed appropriately. A podium works best versus sitting in a chair.

7. Consider providing handouts, news releases, and digital media if applicable.

8. As media arrives, allow them time to set up mics and cameras. This is where a mult-box comes in handy.

9. Law enforcement leaders should wear a class-A formal uniform or professional business attire with a coat and tie.

10. Anticipate the interview to be broadcast live and live-streamed.

11. Press conferences require extensive preparation for the speaker(s). Use the FACTS method, review the messaging cube, and make notes. If the press conference deals with a high level of community scrutiny, potential misconduct, or other complicated situations, consider a well-written, scripted statement that can be read. Reading from a script, paper or digital, requires practice to pull off professionally. There is an art to being familiar with the contents and just glancing at the script, then looking at the audience while conveying the message.

12. Check your appearance before the conference (hair, teeth, clothing, uniform).

13. Avoid distractions (pens, smartphones, smartwatches, ringers).

14. Always anticipate questions, including surprise ones. Assess the community temperature, which may provide insights into potential questions.

15. Run a mock interview with a peer before the press conference.

16. Have a formal approach to the press conference location. Have a strategic communication advisor introduce the speaker(s), provide the ground rules, and remind everyone to silence their phones. As the speaker takes the podium, assume the cameras are recording and the mics are hot.

17. Provide the opening statement (brief) and go into your sound bite and key messages.

18. Maintain eye contact by slowly moving your head side to side naturally to appear that you are addressing all media.

19. If outdoors, try and control the location, especially if it will be nighttime. It's completely fine to suggest an alternate location that has power and appropriate lighting.

20. Keep sentences and answers concise. Circle back to key points as needed.

21. Correct yourself if you say something in error.

22. Take questions. You can bridge difficult questions by reverting to your key points and sound bite ("While it would be premature to speculate at this point of the investigation, what I can tell you is....").

23. Remain outwardly calm and in control. Don't get mad at difficult questions. Watch your facial expressions and nonverbal cues.

24. If you don't know the answer or cannot say it, acknowledge this. Remember, "no comment" is a comment.

25. Have an ending strategy (a colleague can stand in the back and raise a hand to signal time to wrap up with two more questions).

26. Have an exit strategy that is graceful as you walk away. Avoid questions that are shouted at you once the interview has ended. You can remind reporters that you will work on obtaining any unknown information that is publicly releasable and get back to them.

27. Determine if you will respond individually to reporters needing follow-up or schedule an updated press conference (the latter is typical for dynamic incidents).

28. Watch a recording of the press conference and critique yourself. You can also ask reporters and media for feedback.

KEYS TO GREAT MEDIA RELATIONS

- Credibility is key—tell the truth.
- Be courteous and tactful.
- Don't lose your cool.
- Keep your promises.
- Be accessible—the leader should be accessible also!
- Handle exclusives carefully—don't alienate other news organizations.
- Bad news has a limited shelf life.
- Unfavorable news sometimes happens in our line of work.
- The odd, unusual, and extraordinary make the news.
- Be relevant and current with your story pitches.
- Work news desks when disseminating news releases (Call them, as they get hundreds of emails daily).
- Speak plain language and avoid jargon and acronyms.
- Ask for help when you need it.
- Don't be afraid to ask the reporter or news station what their angle is.
- Recognize that occasionally, you will get burned by a reporter.
- Talk through issues with news stations and avoid icing them over.
- Pick your media battles with care.
- Watch other law enforcement leaders, strategic communication advisors, and PIOs when they go on camera (for good and bad).
- Gain technical knowledge by riding with the media, touring the news station, and attending news meetings.
- Do mock interviews so you are prepared.
- Host media mixers to get to know newsroom personnel.
- Get basic equipment—backdrop, podium, mult-box, camera, mic, headphones, and lights.

- Invest in a media monitoring service.
- Host weekly meetings early in the week to forecast potential stories (run your communications like a newsroom).
- Create a media distribution list and understand news cycles.
- Determine how the media will get ahold of you.
- Determine how you will be notified of incidents that may garner media attention.
- Develop news release and media advisory templates.
- Develop a media relations guidebook.
- Develop strategic communication and crisis plans.
- Establish a media relations policy (what is releasable and what is not).
- Ensure you will have access to scenes, videos, and commanders.
- Ensure employees get news releases, media advisories, and stories that will be front-page news before the world knows.
- Have a plan to handle open records/FOIA requests for employee names and photos.
- Train a backup.
- Insist on being a direct report to the leader as a strategic communication advisor/PIO.
- Take care of photographers in the same manner you interact with reporters.
- Having a good relationship with media on the front end buys you time on the back end.
- Participate in regional PIO groups, national organizations, and conferences (Create a regional group if one doesn't exist).
- Take pride in upholding the nobility of our profession.
- Try to have fun and know that your job in communication is critical in the twenty-first century.

PERFECT PITCH TO NEWS ORGANIZATIONS

To increase your probability of getting a story picked up by news media, here is a system that I developed over the years with the aid of advice from reporters and colleagues:

- **P**itch—Prepare a news release that is clear, concise, and easy to understand. Pitch it to news desks and individual reporters. Personalize the pitch so that your agency stands out from other departments in the market.

- **I**ncorporate—Incorporate the key points and a sound bite. Don't overcomplicate your story idea. Due to competition with breaking news and hundreds of other news leads, your point cannot be hidden or buried. A perfect pitch has all the main points in the first paragraph.

- **T**ell—Tell a compelling story. Give the media a great reason to cover this story. Review the ten elements of news value to ensure your story will resonate.

- **C**oordinate—Coordinate visuals, documents, and people to enhance the incident or event. This means having video available, as appropriate. Dashcam, body camera footage, and surveillance video make great story elements. Arrest warrant affidavits also help tell the story.

- **H**ound—Hound them (respectfully) by calling the news desks and reporters to sell your pitch again on the day of the incident or event. For example, if you sent the release on Friday announcing a big press conference for Monday, call in reminders on Monday morning.

INTERVIEW CHECKLIST, PRESS CONFERENCE CHECKLIST, NEWS RELEASE TEMPLATE, AND MEDIA ADVISORY TEMPLATE ARE AVAILABLE AT WWW.POLICEPIO.COM.

MEDIA GUIDEBOOK TEMPLATE— BOISE, IDAHO POLICE DEPARTMENT

The purpose of a guidebook is to establish clear lines of communication between the media and the department. This can be a printed publication disseminated to individual reporters, an electronic version emailed to news desks, or something posted on the agency's website. Boise is a great example. The guidebook is available at https://www.cityofboise.org/departments/police/media-guide/.

BLUEPRINT: MESSAGING CUBE

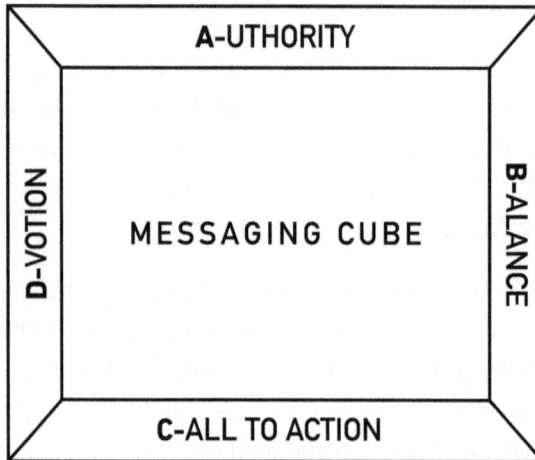

A-UTHORITY

D-VOTION

MESSAGING CUBE

B-ALANCE

C-ALL TO ACTION

CHAPTER 4

LEVERAGING SOCIAL MEDIA

At its basic premise, social media is an opportunity to network through websites and mobile applications. People can share stories, videos, pictures, and other content. While the sheer number of existing platforms can overwhelm leaders and advisors, it can allow agencies to engage authentically with facts and show law enforcement's human side.

The power of social media was on full display when a pit bull named Chance got a second chance at life in 2014. A photo of a police sergeant with the dog in the back seat of a marked unit and a story on how the two became acquainted have generated over thirty-six million views. It was a simple story. The sergeant had been dispatched to a "vicious" pit bull roaming a neighborhood. The initial call had the sergeant returning the dog to its owner. Within a few days, another call came in. Again, the dog was described as mean—a category many pit bulls may get lumped into. And as luck would have it, the same sergeant was dispatched to the second call. Only this time, the owner decided he couldn't care for the dog.

The sergeant decided to adopt the dog himself. The animal shelter was overcrowded, and he figured it must be fate that the two met again. It was a great story, but more importantly, it came at a time when police officers had been involved in several shooting incidents with dogs across the region. Leaders and strategic advisors know that shootings involving four-legged friends are poorly received in a community. This means the story had relevance and enormous news value. The result was hundreds of thousands of shares, positive comments, and likes. People worldwide sent commending letters to the department.

While not originally intended to be a big deal, this story became a viral post for a compelling reason—it showed humanity at its finest. While psychologists claim that society is drawn to conflict and disaster in stories,[20] my experience is that people sometimes crave positivity. It also reminded me not to underestimate the power and influence of social media. Let's look at some proven strategies as the social media landscape evolves.

SOCIAL MEDIA

Social media has been a game changer for the law enforcement profession. While the wheels of bureaucracy turn slowly in policing, since the late 2000s, agencies have increasingly turned to social media to enhance recruitment efforts, identify suspects, and showcase law enforcement activities and work. Many agencies struggle with how to do it effectively.

THE GOOD

Social media has allowed agencies to broadcast important information and brand their respective departments through an amplified digital voice. Here are a few positives:

- Social media is free (for the most part).
- Social media is instantaneous.
- Social media enables you to reach vast audiences.

- Social media lets you control your messaging, which you can tailor to reach various audiences.
- Social media allows you to be proactive.
- Social media can be managed from anywhere in the mobile environment.

THE NOT SO GOOD

As with anything in technology, social media is not without challenges or controversy. Focus on the "good" items above to keep a healthy perspective on the "not so good" list below:

- Social media occurs at all hours of the day and night, challenging a social media coordinator/leader/strategic advisor to keep up with messages and comments.
- Social media requires content moderation to ensure people are not being abused and threatened online.
- Social media requires nurturing and continual development to stay relevant, current, and engaging.
- There is no accuracy filter when others talk about your brand, agency, or officers. This has a negative effect when other people read misinformation or untruths about your agency. Unfortunately, people believe things they see on social media.

THE BAD

Although the positives may outweigh the negatives, a few bad things have surfaced in recent years:

- Lack of civility and plain meanness with some users.
- Anonymity allows keyboard warriors to say things they otherwise would not if their true identities were known.
- Trolls and bots can overwhelm an agency with organized efforts by malicious actors.

WHERE TO START

Agencies should approach social media strategically—what do you want to accomplish? Who do you want to reach? How does social media complement your strategic plan and goals? Let's use the w's and h approach to determine how to position your department on social media.

STEP 1—WHO
Who are you trying to reach? Who is your audience? Who will manage your platforms? Who will respond to messages? Who will be responsible for producing refreshing content? Who will manage social media after hours and on weekends? Who will cover when the content manager is on vacation?

STEP 2—WHAT
What content do you develop? Are you posting a single photo or a collection of pictures to tell your story? What about using video? The "what" is the content that is used in visual and audio storytelling.

STEP 3—WHEN
When should you post? Is there any truth to an advantage to posting at certain times of the day or night? When should you respond to comments?

STEP 4—WHERE
The next question is where to post. Do you use Facebook, or do you post on X (formerly Twitter)? Do you cross-promote across all your platforms? What are the platforms you should be on? Based on who your audience is, which site affords the best value that reinforces your strategic brand? The goal is not to be the agency on a dozen or more platforms. That's referred to as the shotgun approach. Be strategic about platforms. This

takes some research. Some platforms are better suited for different audiences. Also, the more sites you deploy, the more time is required to maintain them.

STEP 5—WHY

The why is important when adhering to a strategic communication plan. If, as an example, you embark on a recruiting campaign, the "why" will lead you to create graphics and videos that support recruiting. Asking why provides an easy way to stay on task.

STEP 6—HOW

How do we create graphics? How do we post? How do we measure success? How can we get officers to send us photos and videos? The how is one of the most important aspects of managing social media.

COMMON SENSE

The person in charge of social media needs political acuity, emotional intelligence, and plain ole common sense. These attributes instill awareness of what is appropriate to post and when it's appropriate to post and can help ensure that the content resonates with your audiences.

COMMONLY USED PLATFORMS IN LAW ENFORCEMENT

Here are some social networking sites that are commonly used in public safety departments across the country. Each platform has strengths and weaknesses. Be strategic and review these platforms with a mind to how they will position your agency to brand, communicate, and build trust with your intended audiences. Some audiences may only be primarily on a certain site compared to other sites.

Facebook, now boasting almost three billion users, is the largest social media platform in the world.[21] While Facebook users are divided evenly among genders, most users over forty become more active as their age increases. Photos, videos, and stories can be posted on this platform.

Instagram, owned by Facebook, has surpassed the two billion mark.[22] A younger demographic can be found, emphasizing those under the age of forty. Photos, videos, and creative content can be posted on this platform.

X has experienced much change in recent years. Boasting about eighty-one million users in the US, this microblogging site is used by many journalists. You can post photos and videos. A recent analysis suggests that 63 percent of X users are between the ages of thirty-five and sixty-five, and 42 percent represent the age group of eighteen to twenty-nine years old, with men making up nearly two-thirds of the audience.[23]

YouTube is the world's second most popular search engine, followed by its parent company, Google. A whopping 74 percent of American adults report using YouTube.[24] Showcasing your agency videos on YouTube is a must.

What about teens? While TikTok has garnered a lot of recent news related to its Chinese connections, it is still on top of the charts, with 48 percent of American users between the ages of ten and twenty-nine.[25] Snapchat also remains competitive with people younger than the age of twenty-five. Whether your agency decides to market to teens is a decision that should be based on your strategic communication plan and what the team wants to accomplish. There are many reputable tutorials on leveraging these networking sites if that's your agency's direction.

Keep in mind what works in one agency may not work in another. Have a plan. Think strategically. Accomplish your goals.

MY STORY AND EXPERIENCE

When implementing social media in Arlington, the agency started small by creating a Facebook page for recruiting in 2009. Then, it utilized the network to assist with hosting Super Bowl XLV in 2011. The agency quickly found that the public began following, liking, and commenting on the posted content. Arlington added Twitter to the portfolio, focusing on pushing critical information to the community to help solve crimes and keep citizens informed. Twitter also allowed our team to connect directly with news media.

The agency was the first in the country to create a "virtual ride-along" experience on Twitter, coining the term "tweetalong." The agency also created a YouTube channel. Eventually, Instagram was added to reach a younger demographic.

While the underlying goal was to reach our community, all these additions to our communication strategy were not equally supported across the organization. Cops were suspicious of social media then; many thought this new approach was a waste of resources. As time passed, the public supported the agency on the platforms, detectives identified suspects through social media tips, and police officers began to embrace this new space. This didn't occur overnight. It was purposeful and required a steady stream of engaging content to change minds and attitudes internally.

Overwhelmingly, the public was on board. The agency was now in an advantageous position to reinforce its brand. More importantly, social media allowed agencies to humanize their officers and deputies. Community members saw police officers as everyday citizens who protect and serve.

As with most things in policing, agencies need to develop a strategy to harness the real power of social media. It needs to be incorporated into your overall communications plan. Social media requires nurturing and attention to increase the probability of success. It requires time to cultivate and create compelling content. It also takes time to monitor and respond to comments and messages. Allowing citizens to interact on a personal level with the department makes everyone feel like they are part of the public safety team.

SOCIAL

Our framework to guide our engagement on social media will center around six main concepts.

- **S**trategy—Our posts and content should reinforce our goals and objectives to achieve our strategic communication plan. Nothing should occur without strategic thinking.

- **O**utreach—Our posts and content should invite two-way communication as an additional outreach tool. Social media enhances our citizen outreach efforts through positive interactions with our audiences.

- **C**reativity—The best posts and content development are creative—graphics, photos, videos, stories, and other ways to invite people to click and interact with the post.

- **I**nform—Most posts and content should usually aim to inform people rather than entertain. For the most part, you should educate your community on what the agency is about. This, in turn, humanizes your officers.

- **A**ctions—Some posts and content ask the public to do something. Maybe it's to help solve a crime, avoid an area due to a road closure, or attend a community event.

- **L**egitimacy—All posts and content should increase the trust and legitimacy of your agency. If the post does not, don't post it. Being open and honest with negative news about the agency will build trust.

Social media content advisors should analyze each of their posts and determine what elements of the SOCIAL framework exist. The more elements, the better. If a message doesn't adhere to SOCIAL, then carefully analyze it to determine if it should be posted.

OFFICIAL SOURCE

One of the biggest advantages of social media is that, as a governmental agency, citizens take what is posted as official and credible. This allows departments to be proactive and break their news. It will enable leaders to tell their stories often. It removes being reactive or behind the curve disseminating information.

CONSISTENCY, CONTENT OVERLOAD, AND THE ALGORITHM

Communities like consistency. Creating and publishing consistent content increases an agency's reach and followers. Posting multiple times daily is not required, and social media managers must find their own groove. A good rule of thumb, especially when starting, is the "1AD" approach—one quality post daily that furthers your strategic plan and goals.

Social media networks contain an algorithm. The algorithm is a set of rules that rank content across a site.[26] This determines what is displayed on a Facebook, Instagram, or X feed or timeline. Every time users refresh their feed, the algorithm works behind the scenes and arranges the content according to a proprietary set of rules and weighted measurements.

I once saw a city post about a dozen content pieces daily on Facebook. I remember thinking that their content manager must have a lot more time in the day to post content than I did, while also thinking their efforts were being wasted due to the algorithm; if you overload your platforms with too much content, previous posts will be buried.

In rare cases, there could be some strategy for overloading a timeline. For example, if a post that caused a stir or a negative piece of content is lingering on the platform, there may be some advantage to bury the post with new content intentionally.

What does matter is the quality of the post. Quality can be represented by enriching posts with photographs, engaging video content, and other items that draw in communities to read and interact with the content. Remember, quality over quantity.

RAINY DAY POSTS

Agencies will have days with abundant content to post. Instead of overloading a social networking site, save the extra posts for a rainy day. They can be used when the time is right or you run out of other content ideas.

CONTENT CREATION

Marketing professionals often quote New York Times bestseller Jay Baer, who said, "Content is fire. Social media is gasoline."[27] Agencies must create relevant and current content, inform and educate, and help promote the basic tenets of public safety.

You don't want to have a void on your platforms. Social media needs fresh content. As you start to create content, focus on your strategy and plan. Everything we do should be intentional and not haphazard. Without purpose, your generated content will not net the desired results.

CONTENT TYPES

Content managers and leaders should focus on topics reinforcing branding and adhere to the strategic communication plan. Agencies that only post police-centric topics miss opportunities to humanize officers and build relationships. Everything from weather posts to good stories involving animals and highlighting the local Little League sports team will generate positive interactions and drive traffic to agency pages. Think outside the box and find and learn from a police department that has mastered the mix of posting broad, generalized topic areas to increase engagement.

Remember, content that builds trust and support from across your jurisdiction is the goal. I love social media influencer Shane Baker's quote, "The goal of social media is to turn customers into your personal evangelist."[28] Customers are those we serve. Personal evangelists are community members who advocate for us and partner with our agency to bolster public safety.

A great story, combined with a photo, can generate community buzz. A short video with a great headline that invites users to watch it can also enhance your content value. Some agencies have content types aligned with certain weekdays— Traffic Tip Tuesday, Wanted Wednesday (or Who's That Wednesday), Throwback Thursday, Furr-ever Friday (pet post), and Sunday Service with a Smile. Use your imagination.

MASTER CALENDAR

It seems that there is a holiday or celebration for everything in the twenty-first century. Agencies should create a master calendar that serves as a guide for posting certain content throughout the year. Leaders should highlight Dispatcher Appreciation Week, National Thank a Police Officer Day, National K-9 Day, and National Donut Day (if you are into silly highlights). Don't forget to highlight your fallen heroes on their End of Watch dates.

CONTENT BRAND AND VOICE

How do you integrate your logo, graphics, vision, or tagline as part of your branding when you post? Voice is also important. Project genuineness and authenticity when posting. The voice should be consistent—this is something to remember when multiple individuals are responsible for social media. Engage in plain speak. Don't read like a news release. Be conversational with the community. Avoid acronyms and police jargon.

Agencies want people to trust their posts. Yes, we also want them to like and share our content. But coming across authentically as the official source of information adds more value.

With attention to voice and plain speak, we can humanize the profession through our content. When done correctly, your community will become strong advocates. Humanizing means to demystify policing and show that officers are just like ordinary citizens, with one small exception—they are the guardians of our communities.

Sure, stories of heroism and bravery lead to extensive shares. But don't neglect everyday posts of officers interacting with neighbors, high fives with kids, and other life moments that project the relational side of law enforcement.

SOCIAL PROOF

This refers to sharing positive feedback and accolades that come in. Citizens will share positive feedback in messaging apps, letters, and phone messages. Sharing commendations creates social proof that your agency is authentic and provides a worthy public safety service. Share these compliments often—screenshot the message, photograph the letter, or put the phone message into an audio or video file, blurring the sender's name if needed.

COMPELLING CONTENT

Everyone knows the difference between a post about an academy graduation and an unposed photo taken by a mom showing a police officer playing basketball with local teens. Leverage compelling content that resonates with your community, reinforces the brand, and aligns with your trust-building plan.

This means making time to be creative. Think about how the post should look to convey the sound bite. Maybe you decide on a video and determine that having different camera angles will create a compelling video product that works better. Find a way to add value, currency, and relevancy that makes the community want to click on the post and interact with the agency through comments and sharing.

Seth Godin reminds us that the analogy of "build it, and they will come" applies only in Hollywood. Social media is "build it + nurture it + engage them...then they may come and stay."[29]

CROSS-PROMOTION

Certain types of law enforcement content can be cross-promoted across all agency platforms. An example would be where the department is looking to identify a suspect. It could post a request for help across Facebook, X, Instagram, and even YouTube if a video were made.

Each social platform generally has its video-sharing service. Content managers should upload video content directly through the Facebook server instead of sharing a YouTube or Vimeo link in a Facebook post. The same is true with other social media networks. It is always best to utilize the native video-sharing system embedded within each social media network to take full advantage of their algorithm.

PRAISE

Doling out praise is a great way to extend the reach of your posts while reinforcing the great work your people are doing. While law enforcement personnel are usually included in most posts, don't forget about providing a shout-out to dispatchers, professional staff team members, office staff, crime scene personnel, clerks, technicians, and other positions. For example, while giving kudos to officers who recovered a stolen car, mention the dispatcher's great job. The public likes to see and hear about the entirety of your operation. Employees appreciate it, too.

THE SPIN FACTOR

Avoid spinning the narrative. To come across as authentic, it's not always roses and butterflies. If the public senses an overtly positive public relations spin, people will unfollow you and write the agency off as unreliable. There's nothing wrong with posting great police work and saving people from burning cars—do that for sure—however, publishing crime trends and topics that don't necessarily reflect favorably on the agency is OK, too. The same goes for unflattering content that becomes public (officer misconduct). Stick to the facts and move on.

WHAT ABOUT POLITICS?

There are no politics in policing, right? I assume you sense my sarcasm. Your agency will occasionally publish content that ruffles someone's feathers. Maybe it's a post about one executive in the department and their unit, which causes other executives and units to feel slighted that you didn't recognize them. Maybe it was an innocent post to thank another organization, only to backfire with negative community sentiment expressed toward the other organization.

Be especially careful when posts include elected officials, especially during campaign seasons. If you do, ensure that all elected officials are represented so there are no darts thrown your way that you are endorsing a particular official.

Agencies can get pulled into politics by accident. Avoiding politics on your social media platforms is the best strategy.

SOCIAL MEDIA ROCK STARS

There are several examples where a particular officer or PIO has obtained social media prominence as the face of their agency. Social media should never be about becoming a rock star for your agency. It can be a hard fall from grace if your social media is built upon one person or group of people. Social media should be representative of the entire agency. If there are any focal points on individuals, it should be focused on the leader. Making the boss look good should be the priority. Because if the "rock star" is more well-known than the leader, Houston, we have a problem. San Mateo County Undersheriff and former Mountain View Police Chief Chris Hsiung said it best in 2019, "Seen a few examples of the PIO fame effect over the years. Doesn't reflect well on the PIO or the agency."[30] I couldn't agree more.

HESITATION BEFORE POSTING

A good rule of thumb to consider before posting deals with hesitation. If you have a piece of content or story and you hesitate for a moment on whether it would be appropriate to post, then you should probably not post it. Once your content is posted, the agency loses control of where that post goes. It's not as easy as deleting something. That's because people will screenshot it.

I like to equate it to a content vacuum. Community members, employees, other agencies, and news media can publish that content across other networking sites. This creates a vacuum where your content is everywhere without your control.

FORECASTING

A good rule of thumb is to run your communications like a newsroom: strategically forecast the current week and the following weeks. At the agencies where I have worked, our teams always met at the beginning of the week to review calendars, events, meetings, and other incidents so we could properly forecast what would be needed.

For example, if the chief will be attending a speaking event, we assign speechwriting, as required, so that the chief is properly prepared. We also assign a photographer. As a chief in my current agency, our senior leadership team meets every Monday morning. Part of the discussion centers around the management of our calendars. If we have a new initiative, we plan how to announce it on social media. If a remembrance ceremony to honor a hero is coming up, we might decide to produce a video to commemorate the event. Forecasting is a good way to plan content for social media.

A leader needs their social media manager in the room as a direct report so they can participate in forecasting. Imagine if one of your midlevel managers in a meeting brings up a good deed performed by an officer over the weekend. Wouldn't it be great for the social media manager to be present and hear this positive accolade firsthand so that a social media post could be created?

AUTOMATED VERSUS SPONTANEOUS POSTING

There can be differing opinions on utilizing platforms to automate a post. Automation is prescheduling a social media post, such as using Hootsuite. Spontaneous posting is publishing content that can be posted on a whim. Which strategy is better? It depends on personal preference. One pitfall with prescheduling is adverse events may take place before the scheduled post is published. A recent illustration was a police department posting a humorous automated post about the weather. However, it was unintentionally published just after a tornado had swept through a nearby community, resulting in allegations the department was tone-deaf.

PUBLIC CRITICISM

Take my word on this. Don't worry about getting some negative comments on your feeds. It's America or the world, for that matter. Not everyone will always agree with you, and certainly, not everyone will like policing. David Alston once said, "Social media is not a media. The key is to listen, engage, and build relationships."[31] As Alston alluded to, once we embrace the three keys, the public criticism becomes less impactful.

ADDRESSING MISINFORMATION

Social media posts are not always truthful. This can cause serious community and organizational harm. Imagine one example: a community member posts an untrue allegation of employee misconduct related to a force encounter. Whether the incident did or didn't occur is irrelevant; other community members who come across the post will form an opinion about the alleged conduct posted.

This highlights the importance of knowing what is being said about your agency in the social media sphere. Monitoring comments, replies, and posts is critical. An agency may be able to institute a social media monitoring plan to assist in capturing negative comments. The organization will then be in a much better position to deal with and respond to inaccuracies as they emerge.

Unfortunately, people make stuff up. Many "viral" posts targeting law enforcement contain grossly misleading headlines and untruths to generate reactions and stir controversy. Society places stock into what they read and see on social media. Departments should confront erroneous posts most of the time.

Agencies can take various approaches when responding to a social media post or video that misrepresents the facts.

The most common method is writing a comment with the agency's official account name to address the misinformation. Another method is bypassing the post in question and publishing a post on the agency's networks. This could be accomplished by creating a graphic titled "Misinformation," "Official Facts," or something similar.

In some cases, you may be able to determine who the poster is. I have experienced some success by reaching out to an individual who posted incorrect information. This can result in the person correcting misinformation or removing the entire post.

Another tool used to determine whether the department should address misinformation on social media deals with reach. If the department sees a false post from someone with two followers, the likelihood of the misinformation becoming a big deal is minimal. If someone with thousands of followers posts wrong information, it may be beneficial for the agency to counter with the facts. Even if the original poster refuses to believe the facts, other community members will hopefully see the agency's response.

SOCIAL MEDIA GROUPS

Your community probably has several community groups. The "All About Insert-Your-Community-Name" groups can garner a lot of followers, which inevitably leads to untruths and misleading posts from time to time. One approach I have found helpful is asking the group moderator if the agency can join the group. This may be a formal request through the Facebook network or an in-person meeting with the organizer. State that your goal is to respond to malicious posts that may harm the community. Reiterate that allowing your agency into the group can help disseminate facts quickly from official channels.

TROLLS AND BOTS

It is worth mentioning that social media may sometimes have hateful people or robots to saturate your feeds with antipolice rhetoric. The Department of Justice announced at the height of the George Floyd incident in Minneapolis that "some of the foreign hackers and groups that are associated with foreign governments are focusing in on this particular situation we have here and trying to exacerbate it in every way they can."[32] According to top law enforcement officials, organized misinformation campaigns by foreign actors and bots are designed to sow divisiveness and discord.

Conversely, trolls may be linked to individuals who hide behind fake profiles or anonymous accounts to attack an agency's social media platforms. The best action is to maintain a robust community content posting policy that adheres to local, state, and federal laws. Leaders can usually borrow a good policy from a top-tier agency that has upheld scrutiny and the test of time. The legislative front continues to evolve regarding whether or when an agency can hide a comment or ban a user. So, it is best to consult with your city, county, or state attorney on these types of cases as they arise. A lot of times, trolls will disappear when you don't respond. In that vein, avoiding negative interactions with trolls is probably best.

CITIZENS WHO QUESTION

As a matter of reference, content managers should not assume every negative comment or post involves a troll or a foreign actor. Quite the contrary, ordinary community members sometimes have genuine concerns and can ask difficult questions. Taking a few moments to respond to a negative comment may change their mind or set the record straight with the actual facts. From experience, there were many times when someone who appeared angry in a social media comment turned around and thanked our agency for clarifying a point. Responding to questions is the right course of action, even if you don't turn them into an ally.

THE CHANGING LEGAL LANDSCAPE

One of the most frequent questions fielded from executives deals with various case law and legal precedents that pop up. It is complicated with different courts with jurisdiction in various areas of the country, so I will keep this simple.

Leaders and advisors should keep up with legal rulings regarding social media in their geographic areas. Most litigation centers on blocking users, silencing or muting users, and censoring speech. I am no attorney. Many departments have legal advisors and attorneys who should be consulted on topics within the legal framework that affect law enforcement's use of social media.

My advice is to adopt a content posting policy, refrain from limiting or removing speech, and activate filters that can sort out profanity and other violations of the terms of use on each social media network. This is to be viewed strictly as a guide only—no legal representation or advice is being conveyed. Check with your legal department or attorney for decisions that your agency undertakes.

For the sake of discussion, there are generally four types of forums related to social media and the First Amendment to the United States Constitution: a traditional public forum, a designated public forum, a limited public forum, and a non-public forum. Leaders and advisors should adopt strategies and policies that do not discriminate based on the viewpoint of a community member that posts in a traditional, designated, or limited public forum.

CONTENT POSTING POLICY AND MODERATION

Most agencies view department social media platforms as limited public forums. The US Supreme Court, as of publication date, has yet to determine the exact public forum as it relates to a governmental entity's social media platforms. This occurs when agencies allow interactions in social media networks where departments operate. Agencies typically limit certain expressive activity through a content-neutral terms of use policy.[33] There are a few examples in the blueprint section of this chapter.

BANNING USERS

Unless authorized in your specific jurisdiction by a higher court or until the US Supreme Court offers guidance through rulemaking, users should not be banned on social media. Again, the First Amendment will provide protections against government censorship based on the viewpoint of a poster. Blocking users does little to alleviate a situation and has enormous legal risks. This is where the bulk of litigation occurs, and governmental agencies have been on the losing end multiple times. In some of the most egregious cases where criminal activity or speech occurs, banning should be a last resort and only with a higher legal approval to protect yourself and your agency.

Remember that, in many cases, other followers will protect your brand, lessening the need for the agency to address negative comments. Bullies that are ignored will sometimes go away. Don't take it personally. Calmer heads usually prevail.

HIDING COMMENTS

Hiding a comment makes a comment hidden from display. However, followers of the account that posted the comment can always see the original comment. Again, this can be murky water in portions of the country. While some agencies apply the "hide" feature to comments that violate the social media content posting policies, users who feel like they have been muted through their comments being hidden have been litigated against agencies.

In one recent case, the National Institutes of Health's (NIH) social media guidelines stated that any comments that contain spam or are improper, inflammatory, off-topic, or offensive would be removed. The NIH would enforce its policy consistently through the hide feature. The court agreed with NIH that its social media pages are limited public forums and that NIH's enforcement of its commenting guidelines by hiding comments through keyword filters was viewpoint-neutral and reasonable. However, the court further stated that if a government social media page does not set restrictions to keep comments on-topic and it opens its social media pages to indiscriminate public engagement, the government page may not hide comments based on viewpoint.[34]

Keep good records of user comments and posts that violate the agency's terms of use before you hide or remove content. Agencies may also report violations of the social networking platform's terms of use to the sites themselves. Most states have a records retention schedule in which posts should be stored.

DELETING POSTS

Like hiding posts, agencies need good screenshots of any post or comment, the reason the post or comment violated the terms of use, and the date and time of removal if you decide to delete a post. Deleting posts and comments should only be utilized when a user posts content that is not constitutionally protected or violates the agency's content posting policy.

VIEWPOINT DISCRIMINATION

Viewpoint discrimination occurs when agencies censor users because they express views and speech with which the agency disagrees. While an agency is not mandated to view or listen to users' speech, implementing an interactive social media space allows individuals to express differing viewpoints. Litigation against an agency will typically center on allegations of viewpoint discrimination when an agency hides, removes, or bans a user based on protected speech. Avoid engaging in disagreements with someone else's viewpoint.

NON-TOPICAL COMMENTS/REPEATED CONTENT

Some agencies incorporate language in their content posting policy that comments and posts are topically related to the agency's particular post. For example, if the agency posts about an upcoming citizen police academy, in theory, a user could not post a use of force video, or the agency could remove it as not topically related to the event. Courts, however, have taken issue with overly broad content rules on social media spaces that are limited public forums.

Posting the same comment on several agency posts represents repeated content. It is unlikely an agency can remove repeated content, absent definable instances where the speech is not constitutionally protected or violates the agency's terms of use. The key to enforcing this is consistency. Targeting an individual that may be construed as viewpoint discrimination will lead to potential legal challenges.

DELETING AN AGENCY POST

A rumor surfaced several years back that law enforcement agencies cannot delete their original posts. This is not correct. Agencies, even in limited public forums, have the right to remove an agency post fully, but remember that this will also remove all the comments. Unless you have an archiving utility software, maintain screenshots and records of the original post along with associated comments to remain in compliance with record retention laws.

TURNING COMMENTS OFF

Some agencies do not allow comments on certain social media platforms. Before you start thinking this is a plausible solution to avoid dealing with issues, go back to your strategic plan. Industry best practices are to build a loyal following of meaningful dialogue, interaction, and two-way communication. Also, be consistent. Don't leave comments on when you have a positive post, and then turn comments off when it's a negative post. Those are not viable strategies and will only lead to community mistrust.

IGNORING COMMENTS AND BAITING

Sometimes, to maintain our sanity, ignoring a sarcastic comment or opinion-based speech that is anti-law enforcement is the best course of action. There may be value in responding with the correct information for erroneous comments. If it becomes a tit-for-tat, the agency can step back and ignore the comments.

Baiting occurs when a keyboard warrior tries to entice the agency into a conversation that cannot be won. Good emotional intelligence should afford you the ability to spot baiting. Don't fall for the bait.

PLATFORM FILTERS

Many social networking sites offer word filters. Enable filters to catch profane and abusive language that violates the networking site's terms of use by automatically hiding those comments. That way, the agency is not even involved in the moderation.

VIRAL POSTS

Occasionally, a post may go viral. A viral post that favors the agency may be welcome. However, most of the time, viral posts have a negative connotation and can lead to thousands of comments. I remember a time when one of our posts reached forty million users. The comments became unmanageable. In those cases, you can only do what you can do. Burying a negative viral post through posting additional agency content may be a viable strategy to move the agency forward.

RATINGS

Under settings, agencies should be able to toggle a button that allows users to leave reviews on your page. With few exceptions, I recommend ratings off. The reason? I have seen and experienced organized efforts to leave one-star reviews during certain situations. Most of the reviewers do not live in your community during these incidents.

SOCIAL MEDIA ARCHIVING

While retention laws may vary across states, most government entities must preserve work product and records. Many companies offer this service for a fee. A software platform or web-based analytical tool connects to your agency's social media networks to capture and preserve all the records associated with each platform. Each service comes with different bells and whistles, but most have some canned reporting along with search functions. It may make sense for some agencies.

SOCIAL MEDIA MONITORING

It's a good idea to monitor social media for what others say about your agency so you can respond to emerging threats to your brand. There are several options, from free sites to paid services. You can also conduct manual keyword searches through the search engines embedded in social networking sites. That will become tiresome and require a lot of patience. Enterprise-level software can give you a limited number of monthly keywords and alerts.

Some of the more prominent players in the industry include Sprout Social, Critical Mention, Meltwater, SocialBee,

Google Alerts, and others. Do your research, talk to your neighboring agencies, and take advantage of free trials before choosing a service.

GETTING PICKED UP BY LOCAL MEDIA

Good reporters and news desks follow agency social media in our fast-paced world. I have had countless stories picked up from posted content. This eliminates having to pitch a story or do a formal news release. As you build your content, consider the possibility of the news media picking it up.

MEASURING SUCCESS

Department heads will measure success in different terms. I believe success hinges on how the public perceives and engages with the agency. This is a qualitative measure. Social media should be a two-way interaction, meaning that managers should post creative content and monitor, respond, and engage with comments. As the level of engagement increases, follower counts and organic reach will also increase.

Departments may look at the number of followers and reach as one metric; however, the style and tone of engagement are more important to consider. They are anecdotal metrics; however, they can be powerful in showcasing positive comments, community buy-in, and support.

Here are a few definitions for leaders and advisors to understand:

- Reach—Reflects how many people your content reached.
- Impressions—Reflects how many times the content appeared on a timeline.
- Likes/reactions/favorites—Reflects engagement activity on who "liked" and interacted with the content.

- Comments—Reflects two-way engagement with the content.
- Shares—Reflects another level of engagement of your content being shared with others.
- Clicks—Reflects how many people went into the content.
- Followers/subscribers—Reflects how many people actively follow or subscribe to future content.

Various commercial programs and monitoring systems measure reach, likes, follows, unfollows, and similar metrics. Social media managers looking for a free way to glance at metrics may turn to monthly email reports that are auto-generated by the various social media platforms. Users can also log into their respective networks and conduct searches related to engagement levels. While looking at a top post from a quantitative viewpoint may provide some insights, it should not be the ultimate sign of success.

RESILIENCY

Social media can be daunting and time-consuming, to say the least. A lot of us wake up to our phone alarms nowadays. And omnipresent on our screens are notifications—likely from social media. Even before we sip our favorite coffee, we are caught in a cycle of scanning social media. It's human nature to want to keep up with society and be in the know.

Growing up, I remember going outside to fetch the newspaper as a hallmark of my morning routine. My parents would have the television on—usually on a particular news station. Why? To find out what happened overnight. Our portable digital devices now put enormous amounts of information at our fingertips. The jury is still out on the healthiness of being connected for our every move.

As it relates to our positions, resilience is something to keep an eye on. Society has developed a new buzzword, "unplugging," reflecting the need to power down our devices, engage in human interaction, and take in nature. In the same sense of unplugging from our personal use of social media, there are times when leaders and advisors need to unplug from the continuous cycle of organizational social media.

Taking a breather can reduce stress. Keep your outlook positive by focusing on the things that you can control. Have a peer network that you can decompress with. Don't be afraid to ask for help on touchy issues that affect your oversight and management of social media.

Dr. Jeff Thompson, a trusted colleague and former New York City Police Department officer, devotes considerable time to resiliency. His book, *warr;or21*,[35] contains strategies to assist when work and life get in the way. He points out that sleep deprivation, poor diet, lack of physical activity, and isolation from others will affect your ability to work effectively and function properly. Check out his work on how resiliency allows you to bounce back from tough situations and incidents that invariably require our attention.

BLUEPRINT—CHAPTER 4

CONTENT POSTING POLICY

A content posting policy aims to establish a code of conduct, rules, and expectations governing the use and participation of social media provided by the agency. Go to www.policepio. com for two example policies: the City of Long Beach, California, and the City of North Port, Florida.

BLUEPRINT: PRO TIPS

- Be aware of what is happening and find relevant public-interest items to share with your audiences.

- Review daily shift reports to find story ideas.

- Build rapport with officers and employees so they will alert you to great story ideas.

- Attend executive-level meetings to listen to what is happening across the agency from an incident and event perspective.

- Be on the lookout for feel-good, humanistic stories that display the positive aspects of policing.

- Remember, law enforcement stories generally captivate a community's interest, so the options for story ideas are numerous (sorry to my friends in the Water Department who must work a little harder to develop content).

- Take photos and build a library of possibilities that reinforce branding and stories.

- Stock your rainy-day fund with extra content that can be used when you come up empty.

- Take videos and share them on social media.

- Approve social media content at the lowest level possible (meaning there should not be a chain of command review process to post on Facebook).

- Remember that the odd, unusual, and extraordinary work great.

- If something gives you pause before posting, avoid posting it (or ask for a second opinion).

- Use humor as appropriate.

- If you preschedule content, remember to turn it off when something happens that would create the impression that the agency is insensitive—be aware of what's happening in your community and the country.

- Highlight commendations and awards.

- Heroism and bravery are solid posts as well.

- Create social proof by highlighting positive accolades directed at officers.

- Break your own news by telling your story first and often on social networks.

- You are the most authoritative source of information in your community.

- Social media has no accuracy filter, so agencies must institute a monitoring plan to know what people say and talk about.

- Address misinformation at the onset to prevent false narratives from expanding across social media.

- Keep an eye on Facebook groups and chat rooms. You will gather a lot of intel on the pulse of the community.

- Reputation and image management are everyone's responsibility in the organization.

- Think outside the box and use broad content (pets, weather, sunsets, sporting events, and other nonpolice topics).

- Never post with text only—use an image, photo, graphic, or video.

- Share more than happy stories—remember, the community wants authenticity.

- Balance criminal activity posts with feel-good stories.

- Be careful about putting booking photos (mug shots) on social platforms—they tend to generate a lot of comments that you have to moderate.

- Don't post things that are not aligned with your agency's culture.

- Answer messages. Respond to comments. Do these tasks timely (Be careful about automated replies to messages—they appear robotic).

- Be proactive versus reactive in messaging.

- Remember, you are in the best position to tell your story.

- Don't go silent during a social media storm. This is when people need to hear from you the most.

- Use the newsroom approach to forecasting stories.

- Use plain language and "Facebook speak."

- Help your community love your department through compelling content. Show your value daily.

- Search for posts where citizens have highlighted your department on their social media feeds—share those, too.

- Don't break the news for another agency on social media (meaning, don't send condolences on X to an agency on a line of duty death when they haven't even confirmed it yet).

CHAPTER 5

INFLUENTIAL BRANDING, REPUTATION, AND IMAGE MANAGEMENT

n the summer of 2020, I joined law enforcement leaders to sit with a local reporter and talk candidly about policing.[36] This interview came amid a troubling time in our country. It was about two weeks after the George Floyd incident in Minneapolis. Communities were reeling. People struggled with how this could happen in America. Good police officers who do the right thing couldn't understand it either. As a profession, we denounced this incident—loudly and clearly.

We discussed our emotions and anger and agreed that our profession must move forward together. Recognizing historical challenges and perspectives in policing, the priority was to make stronger communities. The path to get there was through relationships. Our departments had to tell our story—the nobility of policing. We had to restore faith in the institution of policing. This would be no easy task, given the anger, brokenness, and political agendas. As leaders, we owed it to our people to showcase why policing is essential to public safety. The story of joining the profession to make a positive difference in the lives of others— something that happens every single day in every single agency—had to be told.

One way to accomplish this is through branding. Our goal for the news conference was to recognize that our communities were hurting, acknowledge their peaceful right to protest, advocate for positive change, and reaffirm our commitment to constitutional and relational policing. The interview spoke volumes. I remember receiving feedback from all over the region that the genuineness and frank speaking were a step in the right direction as they related to healing. While the news conference was not labeled as a branding initiative, it became a framework for moving the profession forward. I applauded those leaders who bravely joined the conversation to speak the truth that day—Fort Worth Police Officer Jimmy Pollozani, Grand Prairie Officer Mark Beseda, and Garland Police Lieutenant Pedro Barineau.

BRANDING

Branding is an integral aspect that law enforcement agencies can overlook. While strategic communication is necessary to create, manage, and support the brand, it requires much more methodical processes to maintain the reputational tenets that reflect the nobility of our policing identity.

A brand encapsulates the department name and visual symbols, such as patches, vehicle graphics, and badges, in addition to all the goodwill created by the positive (or negative) experiences of interactions, word-of-mouth stories that reflect favorably (or unfavorably) on the organization, and the people who represent the agency. Notice that I did not say that logos are exclusively the brand. While logos and graphics are elements of a brand that can readily identify an agency, a lot more encompasses a brand.

As author J. N. Kapferer asserts, "It takes more than branding to build a brand."[37] In the business world, this means managing points of contact with clients, products, channels, stores, and employees. In our environment, agencies should think strategically about managing our points of contact—citizen contacts, calls for service, traffic stops, community engagement programs, and so on. We need to be dialed in as leaders on integrating organizational philosophy and service delivery to our brand—i.e., tying our contacts and interactions to the community through strategic communication that promotes the positive side of policing.

WHY SHOULD WE CARE?

Leaders should focus on strategies that build a positive brand for their organization. There are many benefits to a great brand in policing: increase in community support, citizen compliance (translates to less force used), budgetary support, employee satisfaction (less civil unrest and negativity in a community), and external forces (media, politicians, pundits, and naysayers) focus attention elsewhere. A great brand can withstand temporary setbacks, such as adverse or controversial incidents. A strong brand means less rumors and misinformation as the community looks to and trusts the organization as the official source of information.

With increased community support, more people join the department's programs and participate in public safety. There is research that suggests when citizens obey the law, officers can carry out their duties in a manner that relies more on methods that are viewed as procedurally just, thereby reducing the need to use force to gain compliance.[38] Procedural justice is a body of research that focuses on how police and other legal authorities interact with the public through four core principles: treating people with dignity and respect, giving citizens a voice during encounters, being neutral in decision-making, and conveying trustworthy motives.[39] It makes sense that when community members support police, they are more apt to pull over when instructed and comply with officers. A great brand further leads to higher job satisfaction. It's nice coming to work for an agency that enjoys a high level of community support versus patrolling neighborhoods where distrust and noncompliance are commonplace.

BRAND VALUATION

How do we measure the value of our departments? Do we look at tangible assets, vehicles, and the number of gadgets we own? Do we benchmark crime rates against other cities? Do we consider salaries as a measure of value? I would argue that the value of law enforcement comes down to what people think about us. It's all calculated in the hearts and minds of those we serve.

Many chiefs and sheriffs have asserted that their brand is what they say it is. I disagree wholeheartedly with this. The brand is not what we tell people it is—it is what others tell other people it is. The brand is what people say about us on social media—and what people tell their friends it is.

While I concur that executives should try to focus on branding, the valuation of the brand must be measured constantly from a strategic standpoint. Do they feel safe? Do they view us as trustworthy? Do they support our teams? Do they think we are competent? Do they have the confidence in knowing that we will respond quickly to save lives? This all relates to our brand.

When assessing the brand, executives must ask one simple question: how do we want to be known by this community? Everything else can be developed strategically based on this goal.

BRAND IS INFLUENCE

Brands in policing are about influence. It takes considerable time to build, maintain, and protect the brand. And unfortunately, brands can take hits, eroding the ability to influence communities for the better. By the same token, brands can be resilient and withstand setbacks, which will indeed come. The stronger the brand is in a jurisdiction, the better the agency can leverage positive influence in the community.

Don't underestimate a police agency with a strong brand. For example, an agency with a strong brand experiences a controversial use of force captured on a smartphone. With strategic branding, this agency will fare far better through its ability to project calm messages and reaffirm its ability to investigate the facts, compared to an agency that puts little effort into branding, let alone is strategic about branding.

BRANDING IS INVESTING IN YOUR AGENCY

Branding is investing in your agency because your organization. When people land on your website, peruse your social media feeds, and review your publications, do they think your agency is professional? Trustworthy? Is your brand consistent? Your brand elements should convey to the community what's in it for them. Why should they follow you? Why should they want to connect?

Make sure your brand reflects why your department exists. Webpages, social media, publications, and videos should be about what your agency offers the community—through service delivery and programs. Email signatures, business cards, and social media accounts are a few examples and should reinforce ways people can find your agency and engage with you.

The more engagement through branding, the more trust-building will manifest itself.

BRANDING CONCEPTS

For our purposes in strategic communication, I will relate several key concepts of branding in law enforcement:

- Police brands, at the agency and profession levels, can and do evolve over time. Your agency's brand can change in an instant, for better or worse, depending on the circumstances. Imagine a social media post showcasing officers saving a man from a burning car. This will receive tremendous praise. On the other hand, a social media post showing an officer striking someone with a baton, with or without context, can have an immediate negative impact on your brand.

- Your agency's name printed on a shoulder patch represents more than the department's identity. It represents the brand and conveys you are a legitimate law enforcement agency. This is important because it helps when there may be misinformation directed toward your agency.

- The words police, sheriff, constable, trooper, state police, federal agent, and other terms synonymous with law enforcement represent the vow that we swore to protect and serve—part of our brand. It's a trusted promise that people expect from us, which is why policing in the United States is done through consent. It's a privilege we must earn every single day. On the flip side, we are all lumped into the universal brand of "police." This means that although we benefit from good police agencies, we all take a hit from bad policing. One bad apple can have a detrimental effect on everyone's brand.

- Brands in policing evoke mental images and beliefs about the agency when residents see officers in uniform, patrol cars roaming neighborhoods, or hear the agency's name in conversations.

- Law enforcement brands that are influential command a great deal of respect, admiration, and passion for the job officers perform.

WHAT SHOULD WE STRIVE FOR?

We should strive to project a positive brand that people value and want to be supported. An example of this from corporate America is Apple. It is famous as a brand known for superior products that support a premium price, especially with die-hard loyal fans. When a new iPhone is released, a large customer base upgrades based on brand loyalty, regardless of price point. This is the pinnacle of remarkable brand value.

Can this be achieved in policing? I believe so. Agencies that think, act, and communicate strategically command a loyal following of community advocates who will support their endeavors and asks, even amid controversy. Having a strong law enforcement brand grounded in positive values provides space for the organization to operate during tough times. And we will all face tough situations.

WHERE TO START

A strategic approach should be undertaken when determining your agency's brand. Everyone knows that law enforcement provides a public safety service. But how do we provide that service different from our next-door neighboring agency? And how do we project a strong, positive brand that leads to influence? To this end, I have developed a five-step approach to branding.

BRANDING STEPS DIAGRAM

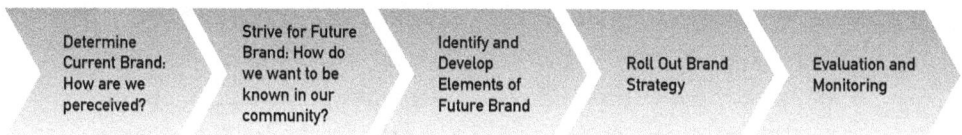

Determine Current Brand: How are we pereceived?	Strive for Future Brand: How do we want to be known in our community?	Identify and Develop Elements of Future Brand	Roll Out Brand Strategy	Evaluation and Monitoring

STEP 1—DETERMINE YOUR CURRENT BRAND

Step one is to ascertain your current brand. This can be achieved through focus groups, interviews, surveys, and listening sessions.

- How are we perceived in the community?

- How do other agencies view us?

- How is our appearance, such as uniforms and vehicles, viewed?

- How do people get information from us?

- How do they report crimes?

- How do they connect?

- How does the community participate?

- What are our mission, vision, and value statements/keywords?

STEP 2—STRIVE FOR FUTURE BRAND

How we want to be known in our community is the underlying question in developing a future brand for the organization. Some questions to consider during step two:

- What does our future look like?

- What strengths and opportunities exist?

- What weaknesses and threats exist that we need to be aware of?

- How do we transition to the future brand that we desire?

- Do we need a new mission, vision, or value statement/keywords?

- What image do we want to project?

STEP 3—IDENTIFY AND DEVELOP ELEMENTS OF FUTURE BRAND

Now that we know what brand we desire, the next step is to develop the identity and visual elements of the future brand. It will be much easier to push a great brand when an agency has developed a brand guide and manual that employees can understand and follow.

- How will people recognize our agency?
- Is there a tagline or phrase that encompasses our future brand?
- Develop a strategic communication plan and crisis plan to protect our future brand.
- Develop a strategic brand manual that issues guidance and rules on how to use the brand elements.
- How can we improve our website, mobile app, and social media?
- What are our email signatures?
- What logos, car graphics, and other symbols do we want to develop?

STEP 4—ROLL OUT BRAND STRATEGY

Once we have developed the brand elements, strategy, and visual identity, we must consider when and how to roll out the new brand.

- Establish target dates to share internally and externally.
- Can we incorporate promotional items to rally employees around the new, refreshed brand?
- Are there bosses or elected officials who need time to be aware of the new brand?
- Can we tie the brand to marketing materials, storytelling, and social media?
- Can we launch with videos?

STEP 5—EVALUATION AND MONITORING

Brands are continuously judged and can change. Continually evaluating and monitoring will enable our teams to respond to attacks and threats to our brand.

- How do we check in with employees to ensure the brand is adhered to?

- How do we monitor our brand in the community?

- How do we know when someone attacks our brand on social media?

- Are there annual surveys that can be disseminated externally?

- Can we capture feedback from business cards during reports? What about after traffic stops?

- Can we apply for trademarks or copyrights related to our brand logo assets?

- How do we change course when we need to?

BRAND ELEMENTS

While agency names, logos, and graphics are elements of brands, a lot more should be considered as brand elements. Think of brands as circular—they are all-encompassing. Much of our service delivery affects our brand. A negative attitude by an employee may convey that the agency does not care. A controversial force incident certainly affects a brand, as does an incident such as officers saving a citizen in a dangerous situation. The way we engage in visual and audio storytelling can affect a brand. News stories affect brands. And social media posts have impacts.

BRAND ELEMENTS DIAGRAM

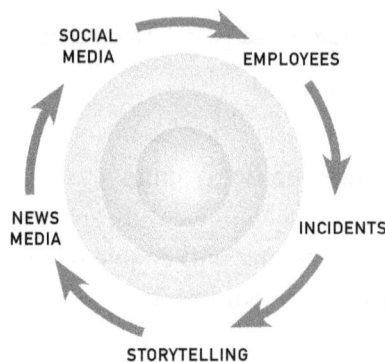

SOCIAL MEDIA — EMPLOYEES — INCIDENTS — STORYTELLING — NEWS MEDIA

WHAT IS A STRATEGIC BRAND?

I will never forget when my previous agency decided to embark on developing a new branding campaign. At the time, we had ten different value words, a convoluted vision statement, and an unclear mission declaration. Most employees didn't know the values or only memorized them by rote when they studied for a promotional exam.

If our employees could not articulate our brand, how could we expect the community to know where we stood as an agency? As an executive team, a committee was launched to review and revise the agency's brand. This was no ordinary committee made up of command staff personnel. It was comprised of individuals across the organization, from line-level officers to the professional staff team members who supported our field personnel. By being inclusive of all segments across the organization, there was a greater likelihood of employee buy-in.

One of the major goals was to ensure that folks clearly understood what we wanted to accomplish. The journey started by reminding committee members that the department needed something that reflected how we wanted our community to know us. What emotions were invoked when a resident saw a police car rolling down their street? How did visitors to our city feel when they saw a group of police officers patronizing a local eatery?

As we met over several weeks, a clear and articulable vision statement emerged that encapsulated how we wanted to be viewed as an agency. The final product, "Service before self, honor above all," reaffirmed to our employees and community the commitment required to provide excellent service. We also centered on three value words: "integrity, compassion, and fairness."

When I came to my current agency as chief of police, we embarked on a similar path to revise an outdated mission, vision, and value statement that no one ever discussed. We wanted to be strategic—with a master plan on how the mission, vision, and values integrated into the brand we wanted. The final theme emerged as "Excellence In Everything We Do." If we could get every employee to believe in this visionary statement, whether they were sworn or civilian or what unit they worked in, our brand would be well conveyed to the community and the employees. The brand is projected across all of our social media platforms, videos, podcasts, and publications.

WHAT'S YOUR ROLE IN THE BRAND?

The role of a strategic communication advisor and leader is to incorporate mission statements, value words, and vision into corporate messaging, both internally and externally, to support the brand. While the leader can set the tone, a great brand is every employee's responsibility.

Think about this example. Most individuals have relatively few encounters with law enforcement. If a police officer makes a traffic stop and treats a community member with substandard service, that community member could perceive the interaction as negative and form the brand image that the entire department does not care about the community. This community member goes a step further and tells their friends. If it's your unlucky day, the community member posts on social media about the negative experience, which further drives adverse brand perception. This is exactly why leaders and communicators need to be dialed in on the importance of branding.

LAW ENFORCEMENT PROFESSION BRAND

In 1955, "To Protect and Serve" was adopted by the Los Angeles Police Department following a contest to create a new motto.[40] Many departments have embraced the same or a similar visionary statement, which is significant in defining the brand of American policing. There may be differences in service levels and how public safety services are provided from agency to agency, however, the distinct purpose is protecting lives and property through policing the community.

As leaders, connecting with residents, visitors, and businesses is more important than ever. A strong brand affords community members the knowledge of how we can assist them, how they can help us, and the types and levels of service we provide as an agency. Even incorporating brand elements into social media posts and videos distinguishes the agency as a credible and trustworthy organization that communities will lean on.

PUBLIC TRUST

Public trust is the bedrock foundation of law enforcement. Without trust, policing suffers and becomes more difficult. The Pew Research Center routinely conducts polls surrounding In 2018, 78 percent of respondents reported having a fair amount of confidence in law enforcement to act in the public's best interests. By 2021, that number had declined to 69 percent of respondents.[41] There could be many reasons for the decline, most notably high-profile deaths of minorities by police. Indeed, a June 2020 poll by Date for Progress found that 37 percent of all voters and 64 percent of Black voters indicated that recent events had made them less likely to trust police.[42] This confirms the extreme importance of bridging the gap between all segments of our communities and the police.

% of U.S. adults who have ____ of confidence in the following groups to act in the best interests of the public

● A great deal   ◐ A fair amount   ○ Not too much/No confidence at all

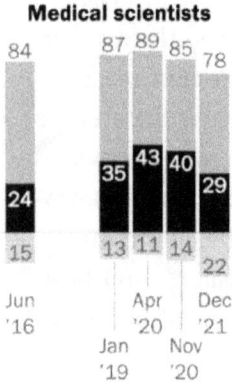

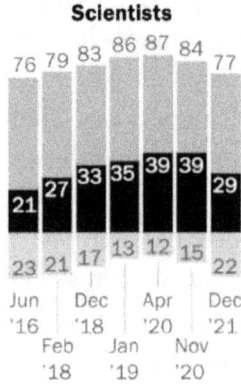

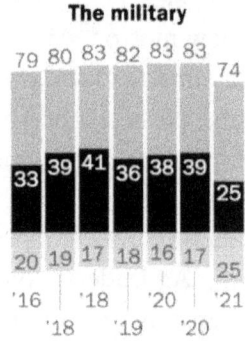

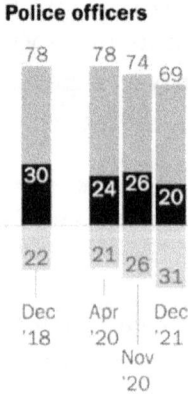

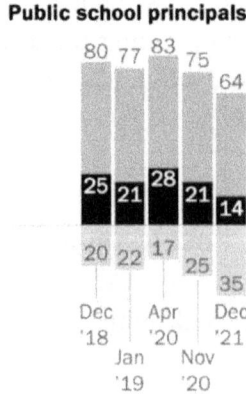

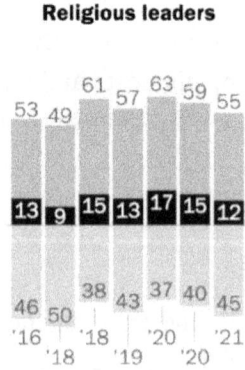

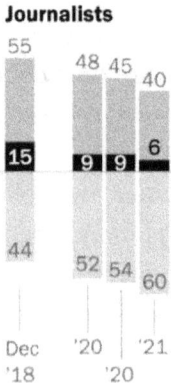

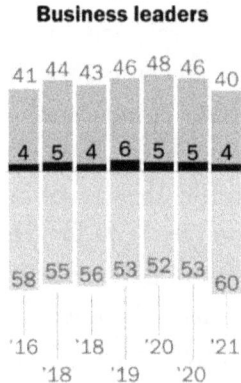

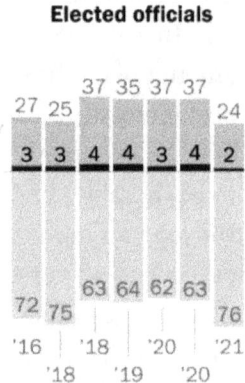

Medical scientists

	Jun '16		Apr '20		Dec '21
A fair amount	84	87	89	85	78
A great deal	24	35	43	40	29
Not too much	15	13	11	14	22

Jan '19   Nov '20

Scientists

Jun '16	Dec '18		Apr '20		Dec '21
76	79	83	86	87	84	77
21	27	33	35	39	39	29
23	21	17	13	12	15	22

Feb '18   Jan '19   Nov '20

The military

'16		'18		'20		'21
79	80	83	82	83	83	74
33	39	41	36	38	39	25
20	19	17	18	16	17	25

'18   '19   '20

Police officers

Dec '18	Apr '20		Dec '21
78	78	74	69
30	24	26	20
22	21	26	31

Nov '20

Public school principals

Dec '18	Apr '20		Dec '21
80	77	83	75	64
25	21	28	21	14
20	22	17	25	35

Jan '19   Nov '20

Religious leaders

'16		'18		'20		'21
53	49	61	57	63	59	55
13	9	15	13	17	15	12
46	50	38	43	37	40	45

'18   '19   '20

Journalists

Dec '18	'20		'21
55	48	45	40
15	9	9	6
44	52	54	60

'20

Business leaders

'16		'18		'20		'21
41	44	43	46	48	46	40
4	5	4	6	5	5	4
58	55	56	53	52	53	60

'18   '19   '20

Elected officials

'16		'18		'20		'21
27	25	37	35	37	37	24
3	3	4	4	3	4	2
72	75	63	64	62	63	76

'18   '19   '20

BRAND PROTECTION

Your brand will inevitably take hits. Many factors can influence the brand, such as critical incidents, controversial force encounters, deficiencies in customer service, negative incidents occurring at your neighboring agencies, and even large-scale national incidents that give credence to misconduct or unlawful force allegations. A strong brand will mitigate and weather temporary setbacks and storms. This is why every employee has an inherent responsibility to protect the brand. Every interaction has the potential to influence the brand positively or negatively. Leaders should discuss the brand and include branding conversations in meetings and training with all employees. The more knowledge employees have on the importance of brand, the better prepared they will be to support and defend the brand.

Leaders should consider the fact that policing takes place in a fishbowl. Everyone is always looking at the actions of police officers, good and bad. This is why officers arrested for offenses such as drinking and driving make the news. It deals with the trust bond that appears to have been broken when an officer, who should be beyond reproach, stumbles. The quicker our profession realizes the fishbowl concept, the more our employees will make better decisions.

One quote that reigns truer today than ever comes from Dr. Stephen R. Covey, "The actions of any police officer, in an instant, can affect an individual for life, and even a community for generations. Given this realization, every police officer must be centered on what is important."[43] This statement emphasizes the relevance of branding in the law enforcement profession.

TRADEMARKS AND COPYRIGHT PROTECTION

In Arlington, I recommended maintaining trademarks and copyrights on various brand elements—all patches (old and new designs), badges, car graphics, and other identifying elements. Registering your visual elements with the United States Copyright Office gives an agency some legal recourse when their elements are used without permission.

The importance of this was demonstrated at the height of the Grand Theft Auto video game craze. Our agency started seeing Arlington police cars used in the game as "skins," which caused serious brand issues. With our nifty copyright protection, our city attorney could send a cease-and-desist letter to users who were utilizing our logos, patches, badges, and car graphics.

This also came in handy when a community member created fake "wanted" bulletins with the names of officers who had allegedly wronged the community member. Again, a not-so-nice legal letter was sent, resulting in the person removing the fake bulletins from social media.

Some costs are associated with filing for trademarks and copyrights, but it is money well spent. Keep an eye on the expiration of the trademarks and copyrights, as the agency will have to renew every couple of years.

BRAND TOOLS

Here are some time-tested approaches to managing media, creating social media posts, and branding an agency.

CREATING VISUAL ELEMENTS

Create visual elements to project and reinforce the brand. This may include graphics, tag lines, and other identifiers that can be attached to your content. Many software packages, third-party vendors, and YouTube "do-it-yourself" videos exist. Content managers can also attend training seminars.

One of the ways I found success was by replicating the work of peers across the country who found unique and innovative ways to reinforce their brands. An example was connecting with Sarasota, Florida, Police Public Information Officer Genevieve Judge on how she created their holiday videos synchronized to commercial music. She shared her secrets, allowing our team to replicate a way to humanize our officers and build our brand. In my experience, chiefs, sheriffs, and strategic comms advisors love sharing their successes.

Here are a few tried-and-true methods that may work for your team. Utilizing the KISS principle (keep it simple, stupid), I like solutions with the fastest and easiest way to get up and running. These tools will assist you in creating flyers, annual reports, graphics for print publications or social media, and many other products that can be adapted for employees and communities. In each product created, embed elements to keep the community zeroed in on the brand.

TOOLS

So, you have figured out what you want your brand to be. That's great. Here are some software, mobile apps, and branding tools to create and reinforce your brand. As a disclaimer, no commissions are made if you choose any of the tools we highlight.

CANVA

This app simplifies graphic design for novices across iOS and Android platforms. The company also has a web-based platform that adds some functionality. While some features are available in their free platform, the paid service is really where the higher-end functions exist.

The Canva user interface is intuitive. There are thousands of professional templates, images, and other content that can get you up and running in a short time. Team collaboration is available for users in a larger environment. One of the features used most is their precise social media template sizing. Their templates correctly size the content so that it looks great on each social media platform. Many police departments have created full magazine-scale annual reports with Canva. Infographics are also easy to manipulate and render for social media and print products.

MARQ

Formerly known as Lucidpress, Marq is a web-based online editor that can create stunning graphics, social media posts, annual reports, flyers, and every other print product that one can imagine. You pay an annual fee based on the number of users and storage needed. Compared to some of the other print publication products on the market, Marq has an easy-to-learn, intuitive interface that can demystify desktop publishing and bring the agency's professionalism up a notch. There are thousands of templates available through their website as well.

The largest benefit to the program is that the user is not required to install proprietary software on a native device; as a web-based program, you can log in on any device from anywhere. It is my "go-to" platform for desktop publishing and consistently produces professional and beautiful publications and social media graphics.

AFFINITY

For those who despise the annual subscription fee model, Affinity may be your answer. Affinity Publisher, Affinity Photo, and Affinity Designer compete directly with Adobe InDesign, Adobe Photoshop, and Adobe Illustrator. The learning curve is a little more challenging than Marq, however, and the software must be installed directly on your computer.

There is also a large secondary market of templates. Affinity Publisher can even import Adobe templates with certain file extensions. Affinity also allows a user to do a lot more than Marq when it comes to creative design and controls. The best part is that once you purchase the software, it is yours for life, including all the free updates.

ADOBE

Adobe is the publishing and photography industry standard. However, Adobe may not be for everyone. Most of their products—InDesign, Photoshop, and Illustrator in particular—have steep learning curves and require lots of studying to accomplish basic tasks. There is also the annual subscription fee that is usually necessary to access the full range of features. Adobe Lightroom CC and Lightroom Mobile are very easy programs to quickly enhance a photograph that may be used on social media. If you have the time and skill, Adobe creates the most stunning products.

MOBILE APPS

Mobile apps have made it easy for agencies to create quick graphics and posts that reinforce the agency's brand. Thousands of apps get the job done. Here are a few tried and tested ones that I have used.

UNION

Union was one of the early apps on the market that allowed users to attach a PNG graphic (fancy phrase for a transparent image with the background removed) to a photograph. While the app boasts many uses, it makes it easy to combine images, brand your posts, and push out blended graphics. The app allows users to apply masking, add brushes to adjust images, and create nice compositions to enhance their story. Add your patch or badge to brand the post or photo.

PIXELCUT

The pro version of this app allows you to quickly remove a background, erase unwanted things in a picture, and use various templates and tools.

PHONTO

This app provides a fast and easy way to add text to an image with various fonts and colors. Resizing text is simple with the touch of a finger.

MAGICERASER

Like PixelCut, this app allows users to remove backgrounds with a touch.

PICCOLLAGE

This legacy app allows users to create cool graphics and backgrounds. Agencies can add multiple graphics, photos, and text to create posters and social media content.

BLUR PHOTO BACKGROUND

This app helps agencies quickly blur faces, license plates, or unwanted objects in a photo to comply with public information laws.

IWATERMARK

This mobile app can store your PNG graphics for quick branding. Everything from a patch, badge, or logo can be stored for instant watermarking of photos and posts.

RETOUCH

This app provides a fast way to remove distracting objects in a photo. If you have ever wanted to remove a light pole or unsightly trash can, this app is for you.

STOCK IMAGES

Agencies may need a stock photo. While some mobile apps, services, and software platforms offer free options, there are also paid services. Adobe Stock, Shutterstock, and iStockPhoto are a few of the big players in the market.

AGENCY IMAGES

It is always best if an agency can devote some time to go out and shoot their own photos and videos. By having a library of several good images that can be stored on your mobile devices in a folder devoted to graphics, one can easily prepare social media posts. It is also a great idea to have a network folder on your laptop or desktop containing multiple photo options.

BRAND CAMPAIGNS

Campaigns sometimes emerge—sometimes, they originate internally or may come from an outside organization. The International Association of Chiefs of Police hosts brand campaigns to assist law enforcement agencies. Examples include the "Why I Wear the Badge" and "#PathForward" campaigns. When deciding to create or partner with a brand campaign, leaders need to determine and consider:

- Reason for the campaign. What are we trying to accomplish?

- Who is the target audience?

- Could the community misperceive the campaign?

- Will the campaign lead to mockery or ridicule for the agency?

- Are the campaign or brand keywords already associated with other words, phrases, or hangtags that don't align with the agency's or profession's value system? Worse, would the campaign come across as offensive or have an unintended consequence of backfiring on the brand?

- Don't launch a campaign at a time that may come across as the department being tone-deaf to what is occurring around it.

As with anything, agencies should approach brand awareness campaigns with caution. Leaders should scrutinize campaigns and consider any potential blowback. For example, in 2014, a large metropolitan police department launched a brand campaign on social media asking followers to post photos of officers with a hashtag created by the agency.[44] Unfortunately, many images showed unflattering photos of officers using force, making arrests, and pointing weapons at people. While the agency had intended to increase outreach, there were some challenges with the execution that created several adverse news stories.

In addition to campaigns, our brands need to be agile and responsive to other threats. In one of my agencies, the department published photos depicting a sizable donation made to an injured officer. The original intent of recognizing the donor for their support quickly transformed into a debate on taking gratuities, hence a brand attack. More recently, a local agency in the Dallas-Fort Worth market posted a photograph of several department members posing with a telephone company that provided a free pizza party. This caused a public outcry against the company that donated to the department. Before it becomes public, leaders and advisors should preview content related to campaigns, stories, or posts that may inadvertently cause damage to their brand. While there are times that this may be unforeseeable, it warrants review to protect your brand. Stick to the SOCIAL elements to reduce the likelihood of setbacks.

BLUEPRINT—CHAPTER 5

BRAND CHECKLIST

1—Determine Your Current Brand
Before they figure out where they want to go, leaders need to understand their existing brand. In some rare cases, the brand may not require changes. Executives and strategic communication advisors need to conduct research to determine the current brand.
Conduct: • Internal surveys • External surveys • Interviews • SWOT analysis (Strengths, Weaknesses, Opportunities, and Threats) Establish: • Branding committee • Focus groups (made up of internal and external stakeholders) • Brainstorming sessions • Listening sessions with community groups Review: • Current mission, vision, and values • Current organizational strategic plan (if one exists) • Current strategic communications plan (if one exists) • Current branding manual • Last annual report • Crime reports Prepare: • Executive summary of findings and research • Roadmap to move to the next step

2—Strive For Future Brand
Determine what you do best and how you want to improve processes and functions where you miss the mark. This will help shape the future brand. Executives and strategic communication advisors need to identify the organization's guiding principles and core values (what is most important and why the agency exists).

Conduct:
- Interviews with the executive team
- Interviews with all employees
- Strategic planning retreat

Establish:
- Guiding principles
- Core mission, vision, and values

Review:
- Work completed by the branding committee
- Work completed by other organizational segments related to branding

Prepare:
- Executive summary on go-forward strategy
- Roadmap to move to the next step

3–Identify and Develop Elements of Future Brand

Determine how your agency will visually display and live the brand. While logos and graphics come to mind, remember that this includes how officers carry themselves and perform in the community. Executives and strategic communication advisors must focus on communication tools, audiences, and identity to properly convey the brand.

Conduct:
- Interviews with graphic artists, involved employees, and senior city/county leadership teams

Establish:
- Logo (possibly multiple logos that fit different social networking and print spaces), patch, badge, vehicle graphics, and uniform (includes business uniform standards as well)
- Color schemes in graphic design
- Tag line or saying that reflects the brand
- Website design standards
- Photography collection that reflects the brand
- Video collection that reflects brand (intros and outros)
- Brand design manual that establishes appropriate and inappropriate use of brand elements and symbols

Review:
- Proposals that support the brand (avoid the term "rebranding," as it conveys that something was wrong with the original brand)
- Graphics, symbols, and elements

Prepare:
- Executive summary of work completed
- An organizational strategic plan that reflects/reinforces the brand
- A strategic communication plan that reflects/reinforces the brand
- A crisis plan that reflects/reinforces the brand
- Roadmap to move to the next step

4—Roll Out Brand Strategy
Determine how and when your agency will unveil the refreshed, new brand. Consider the internal rollout to ensure employees rally behind it.

Conduct:
- Meetings with employees (to get buy-in)
- Meetings with senior city/county leadership

Establish:
- Rollout date
- Media strategy to launch brand (consider advance talks with trusted reporters or stations to arrange coverage)
- Social media platforms that coincide with strategic communication plan
- Website unveiling
- Mobile app unveiling (if applicable)
- Approved email signatures
- Prezi, PowerPoint, stationary, letterhead, and envelopes
- Brochures
- Swag material (sunglass cloths, key chains, and other products that reflect the brand)
- Badge, patch, approved graphics, coins, and other items to reinforce the brand
- Any policies and orders to utilize and manage the brand

Review:
- Rollout plan

Prepare:
- Executive summary of work completed during this step
- Roadmap to move to the next step

5—Evaluation and Monitoring
Determine how your agency will evaluate the brand, monitor the brand, and make adjustments as necessary. Reputation and image management are paramount for law enforcement agencies in the twenty-first century. Executives and strategic communication advisors need to continually evaluate the communications landscape to be in a position to respond to a variety of threats to the brand.

Conduct:
  • Reviews of brand launch until acceptance
  • Assessments of brand strategy
Establish:
  • Media monitoring
  • Social media monitoring (CriticalMention, Hootsuite, X Pro, Google Alerts, Mentionlytics, and BoardReader)
Review:
  • First week
  • Thirty days
  • Ninety days
  • Annually
Prepare:
  • Executive summary on work completed during the final step

PRO TIPS

- Branding is everyone's job, not just the leader's or strategic communication advisor's.

- If you cannot articulate your agency's brand, how can employees be expected to?

- Public safety is a universal brand; however, each agency should strategically position its individual value to its community.

- What happens in Vegas does not necessarily stay in Vegas—the policing profession can be affected by things that happen elsewhere.

- A great brand increases community support, citizen compliance, budgetary support, and improved employee satisfaction.

CHAPTER 6

VISUAL STORYTELLING

In 2012, I asked my boss for permission to visit other police agencies that were doing a great job with video-based products. Without hesitation, he told me to write a proposal for site visits with a list of items that would benefit our department. To get maximum benefit from the time away from the office, we developed a travel plan that would include visits to three agencies in the Northeast: Baltimore, Boston, and New York City.

While these were three large agencies, all belonged to the Major Cities Chiefs Association (MCCA), which Arlington also belonged to, which made it easier to get approval. Boarding a plane, I couldn't wait to see the magic that was happening behind the lens. Little did I know this trip would forge lifelong friendships with some of the best innovators in the police public information business.

The first stop was Baltimore. Their agency was producing a daily video series, BPD-TV. Yes, it was daily. It was scripted, well-orchestrated, contained graphics and music, and ran like a mini-newscast. I was amazed at their accomplishments in community education and the number of views.

During this visit to Baltimore, I met five very important people. This resulted in strong bonds, countless networking opportunities, and sage advice when times got tough. The first was, interestingly, on the first day of her new job, the same day as my arrival. Judy Pal, chief of staff for Baltimore PD (BPD) at the time, was a "no holds barred" kind of executive. She always walked with purpose and was extremely competent. She knew how to run communications. From my vantage point, she coined the term "strategic PIO." She introduced herself as she walked to a scene with then-BPD Commissioner Anthony Batts, and we exchanged contact information. Fast forward to today: Judy runs a successful consulting and communications business, 10-8 Communications, and is considered one of the industry's best. Her experience working for some of the largest agencies in policing is impeccable. Our paths regularly cross.

Next on my VIP list, I met with Anthony Guglielmi, Director of Communications for BPD. He had a large, beautiful office and a difficult last name to pronounce, let alone try to spell. He was wearing a suit and tie. Anthony told me that his house was my house and to take anything they did well back to my agency. Years later, Anthony and I had the privilege of serving on the MCCA Public Information Officers Committee and collaborating on executive publications. He served as my co-chair, and together, we achieved many things in the public information field to make policing better. Anthony served in some of America's largest law enforcement agencies—Baltimore, Chicago, Fairfax County, and the United States Secret Service.

Heading down a hallway, I was introduced to Eric Kowalczyk, a sergeant with BPD at the time. Eric is a consummate professional and well-versed in public policy decisions and crisis management. As an accomplished author, his book *The Politics of Crisis*[45] is a great reference point for managing disasters, building community resiliency, and bridging the gap between police and citizens. Eric and I have since collaborated on dealing with tragedies, sharing lessons learned to better prepare for future challenges.

Next on my list was Jeremy Silbert, a down-to-earth police officer who was a primary face of BPD-TV. Jeremy and I hit it off right away. He talked me through the process of producing visual content that worked with community engagement strategies. Through his guidance, our own video series, *Inside APD*, was successfully launched upon my return. Even more than a decade later, some of the simple truths gathered on that trip are embedded in two current video series that I distribute today as a police chief, *WSPD-TV* and *On The Job With Chief Cook*.

Lastly, I met with the guy behind the scenes doing the filming, production, lighting, audio, and editing. Gino Inocentes, the epitome of professional videography, shared his secrets to graphic design, B-roll video (supplemental video that helps guide a story along), and sequencing of shots. I always wanted to hire Gino and bring him back to Texas. Like all these VIPs, Gino has positively impacted our profession.

The next stop was Boston to analyze their video production powerhouse. Then, we went on to New York City. Walking into One Police Plaza can be intimidating. The history of that place is amazing. The NYPD had an extensive video team, and I gained takeaways to assist my agency.

Regardless of the size of your agency, the lessons in this chapter will assist leaders and advisors in creating visual content to educate and engage with communities. Interested in conducting a site visit? Challenge your boss to allow opportunities to visit other peer agencies that are doing videos well. There's nothing wrong with replicating what works and applying the principles learned to your audiences. They say imitation is the best form of flattery.

VISUAL STORYTELLING

Video can be a powerful tool for a law enforcement entity. It opens a world of creativity and allows departments to tell a story using visual elements. There are many reasons to create video content. Internally, video messages from the top can communicate important updates to employees, especially in larger agencies where face time may be challenging or limited. On the external communications front, video can be used to supplement an agency's proactive social media strategy and brand. Consistency is the key to developing compelling content that resonates with followers.

One of the easiest ways to create a video is to start small with just a few pieces of equipment that departments probably already own. While thousands of dollars can be spent on high-end video cameras, it is not necessary for capturing and publishing videos for local government. An old saying says the best camera is the one someone already has with them. Due to the proliferation of mobile telephone technology, shooting high-resolution video is easily achieved on the go.

MOBILE VIDEO

Mobile journalism allows agencies to reinforce positive brand elements. Professional videos can be shot on a phone. There are indie film festivals and Apple product videos that demonstrate the high level of professionalism achievable on a mobile device.

When considering video, think of the policing profession as a business. Corporations spend millions of dollars to reinforce their corporate identity. People are visual learners; for many, seeing a video may take preference over reading a post. Utilizing videos as part of your social media and branding strategy is a cost-effective way to get your message out. It also enhances police legitimacy.

TYPES OF VIDEOS

There are many different types of videos that governmental agencies can create. Videos can promote a new program or service, answer citizen questions, address crime issues, showcase positive work, and provide training. Public service announcements such as burglary prevention messages also fit well on short video pieces. Recruiting videos, documentaries, and in-depth behind-the-scenes pieces do well. For example, capturing moments during National Police Week enables you to talk about the honorable sacrifices made by our heroes.

When determining your video type, it is good to develop a plan. Some videos are simple to produce, some may require more involvement, and some may even be complex, requiring multiple scenes and professional talent. Ask yourself what the storyline will be. Who is your intended audience? Are you trying to entertain or inform the public? Why should a citizen click on the video and watch it? Once you get those answers, the video should have a natural progression and guide the viewer through the storyline.

"Viral" is not a kind of video. Remember that the public is in complete control of how a video performs. Trying to be the next YouTube sensation may result in frustration. Some videos I thought would do well flopped, and others unexpectedly took off with thousands of views and shares. In my experience, videos that achieve viral status have great timing, off-the-wall creativity, and an ounce of good luck.

VISUAL STORYTELLING AND MOBILE JOURNALISM GUIDE

Come up with the story idea. Think of the end first, which will assist in deciding the content, tone, style, and length. Think of the proper sequencing, determining the shots you need for the video. Identify the host and talent.

Will it be a talking head with a B-roll, or will it be a video with narration? For example, if the talent in a studio discusses railroad crossing safety, having a B-roll of a passing train at an intersection would guide the viewer through the story and reinforce what is being said. Speaking of B-roll, always get more secondary footage than you need. It may be difficult or impossible to recreate the same outdoor lighting on another day if you edit the video and need additional footage.

IN-HOUSE VIDEO BANK

Our agencies are full of "routine" everyday video captured by body cameras and dashcams. Create a repository of footage of great interactions that can be used in videos. When my team makes a great felony arrest, I check to see if there is good video. Get to know your public release laws for agency-owned videos as they vary across states.

SCRIPTED OR IMPROMPTU

Scripting or "running and gunning" through a video without a script is your choice. There are advantages and disadvantages to writing a script. Advantages include ensuring you capture all the elements needed to tell the story and you completely understand the video's goals and audience. Disadvantages include the fact that it takes time to script a video properly.

Impromptu shooting carries potential drawbacks, such as forgetting a scene that might need to be included in the video. Time will usually dictate whether you script or just go for it.

SHARING VIDEO

There are many different social networking sites where you can publish videos. While most law enforcement agencies post video content on Facebook, X, YouTube, Instagram, TikTok, and Vimeo, trends evolve, so it's best to continue researching the networks that work well for your community. The main rule of thumb is to post finished video products to each individual platform. In other words, keep YouTube videos on YouTube and do not post a YouTube link to Facebook. Rather, upload the same video directly onto Facebook. The same is true for X, Instagram, and other networking sites.

SOUND

If your audio ends up sounding awful, your video will look terrible. An excellently produced video doesn't cut corners on sound. The good news is that technology has shifted so rapidly that microphones are easy to find. While manufacturers abound, some trusted brands routinely perform well.

DJI is one of my go-to setups. The system contains two transmitters for two-person interviews and one receiver with a nifty charging case that keeps the mics in sync with the receiver. It is completely wireless, and battery life is excellent. There are multiple mounting options with either a clip or magnetic attachment. The touch screen ensures that the operator fully controls the audio options. Not to mention, the kit will only set you back a couple hundred dollars.

RØDE has been a contender for many years in producing great-sounding audio for video projects. My team has used the RØDE Wireless GO II system, although the setup is a little more cumbersome than DJI's. The RØDE kit also contains two transmitters and a variety of Lavalier microphone cords. RØDE also has stick mics, which allow you to attach a flag banner to brand your agency. The RØDE Reporter model has been around for years and gives users an easy plug-and-play experience for various smartphone options.

DEEP-POCKETS AGENCIES

For those with unlimited budgets, feel free to purchase full-frame sensor video cameras with professional mics. Have a camera operator from a local news station teach you the ins and outs. DSLR and mirrorless digital cameras can also take great video and accept microphone inputs.

LIGHTS

When I started creating videos, I did not realize the importance of ensuring my subjects and scenes were lit appropriately. Light setups have many options. After spending lots of money on various lights, I have settled on one primary light manufacturer—Lume Cube. The Lume Cube studio panel lighting kit is battery-operated and produces beautiful light with an opportunity to change the color temperature by turning a dial. The included barn doors allow users to focus and shape the light on their subject. This portable powerhouse will increase the quality and look of your video productions.

Three-point lighting is a simple technique that can be used for most video projects. It involves the placement of three light sources in different positions: a key light, a fill light, and a backlight, also called a rim or hair light. The key light is the primary and brightest light source, set at about forty-five degrees to the camera. This will create a slight shadow on the opposite side of the subject's face. The fill light mirrors the key light on the opposite side of the camera and fills in the shadows on the subject. It will be less bright than the key. The backlight is positioned behind or on the side of the subject, out of camera view, to create a rim of light or outline on the subject's head. This creates separation and dimension from the background.

STABILITY

If you are shooting in a studio environment, it's best to mount the smartphone or camera on a tripod to ensure a stable platform and afford your final video a professional look. For action videos, shooting handheld is completely fine. As you create more videos, you will find yourself in a movie theater or watching streaming videos and noticing different shooting angles you can incorporate into future projects.

VERTICAL VIDEO SYNDROME

There are a lot of people afflicted with V.V.S.—vertical video syndrome. It's easy to cure yourself of this disorder. Hold your mobile phone the correct way when you are shooting video—horizontally. When you shoot video vertically, your video will look like crap. Yes, I know vertical videos are everywhere because people don't realize that while you can rotate a photograph, you can't turn a television screen or computer monitor. Be professional by shooting horizontally.

TELEPROMPTERS

There are elaborate teleprompter setups for full-frame sensor camcorders and smartphones, and mobile apps also work. I use a teleprompter mobile app for most of my videos that require a lot of content. Remember, even if using a teleprompter, make it appear natural so the audience doesn't think you are reading a screen. Also, get plenty of B-rolls to cover the talking head with visuals.

TEMPLATES AND CONTRACTING VIDEO SERVICES

Thousands of templates that offer different looks for videos are available for a fee. Sometimes, I have invested a few dollars in templates to create openers to brand the video. It's your preference whether the value is there for you to spend money on templates. Some companies producing high-end products include Adobe, Motion VFX, Motion Array, and Envato.

Agencies with money can hire a freelancer or company to shoot, edit, and produce video content. Before you embark on this road, realize that the concepts in this chapter are easy to master. As with any skill set, the more videos you create, the better you become. If you are in a pinch and need a video on the fly, a contractor might be the way to go. For example, Fiverr has professional videographers who can assist you in creating the video.

EDITING

Avid was the king of video editing when I first started video production. Unfortunately, Avid has a steep learning curve, and technology continues progressing, allowing video editing on smartphones and tablets. As an Apple guy, I routinely use Final Cut Pro X for heaving lifting, now available for the iPad. Most communication professionals I know use Adobe Premier Pro, which is available for Windows and Mac.Vegas Pro is also a good editor. There are tons of reviews available online. Most software companies offer a free trial. Find something that works for you and your agency, and stick with it.

LENGTH

People have short attention spans. This means we should create short videos for social media. Many videos do great in the thirty-second to two-minute timeframes. Documentaries and extensive stories might run longer. A good rule of thumb is that every minute of the finished product takes one hour to edit.

TRANSITIONS, GRAPHICS, JUMP CUTS, AND MUSIC

Transitions are a creative way to move from scene to scene. They may signify a shift in the storyline, show a passage of time, or move the viewer smoothly into a new scene. Don't overuse transitions. The video should not look like a PowerPoint with all the transitions flying into and out of the frames.

Graphics allow agencies to brand their videos. They may consist of transparent patches, badges, or title bars. Use graphics sparingly to not detract from the storyline.

Jump cuts are edits to a single sequential shot or frame that makes the action abruptly leap forward in time. These need to be covered by a B-roll or a suitable transition. For example, an officer talking to the audience with a jump cut will make the officer's face and mouth look weird and out of sequence without putting a B-roll over the jump cut.

Music can enhance the emotion and feel of the video. Lots of royalty-free music is available for a small fee. Storyblocks and Adobe are my main go-to music sites. Don't use Apple iTunes or Spotify commercial music in your organizational videos. It will immediately get flagged, removed, or, worse, could cause problems for the agency on copyright license agreements. For an annual fee, Storyblocks contains thousands of royalty-free videos and audio files for download to enhance your video (and your podcasts, too).

RULE OF THIRDS

In video (photography, too), the rule of thirds refers to dividing your video frame into thirds, with two vertical and two horizontal lines. The talent and subject elements should be in at least two-thirds of the frame or six of the nine boxes. A good rule of thumb also includes placing the horizon on either the top or bottom horizontal line to create a more eye-pleasing experience for the viewer.

LEARNING

Over my career, the fastest way I learned videography, photography, and editing was simply by seeking out online tutorials and books. YouTube is a good starting place. Watch newscasts and observe how producers and reporters package their pieces together. Partner with some news photographers to show you the ropes. With editing, it takes time to develop skills and comfort. The more you do, the better you become.

HAVE FUN

As you can see, easy ways exist to create persuasive video content. Have fun doing this job. With a little creativity, your organization can humanize officers and deputies, leading to greater community trust.

WEAPONIZED VIDEO

I would be remiss if I didn't mention the potential for some individuals to weaponize video against agencies. I often get questions from leaders about what to do in cases like these. As a topic of training I received at the FBI National Academy in Quantico, the instructor discussed the importance of analyzing community and department videos for the potential to be taken out of context or cause harm due to technological limitations. Most executives and advisors already know that video does not tell the entire story of an officer's decisions, perspectives, or perceptions.

An article published in 2022 by retired Lieutenant Frank Borelli pointed out that body cameras do not always point to where an officer's eyes look.[46] Many cameras are mounted on the officer's chest, at waist level on a duty belt, or even on a shoulder. As an officer takes a bladed stance, the camera may point in a different direction than the officer is looking. Another limitation of body cameras is the sounds the camera records. The audio captured by the camera may be better than the human ear is capable of hearing, leading to a different perspective for the officer. Also, frame rates, motion, and internal computer mechanics can make the video appear different from reality. This is especially true for low-light situations. We had a case in an Arlington officer-involved shooting where the officer's flashlight washed out the video due to the camera aperture initially being unable to filter the light.

As a leader, approach video cautiously—both organizationally captured video and video from the outside world, such as doorbell cameras, surveillance systems, and cell phone captures. By considering these limitations, executives can ensure that video usage policies, use of force reviews, and analysis of evidentiary videos follow a best practice approach that recognizes the constraints of current video systems.

Investing in a video analyzer is one way to protect officers and reduce agency liability from frivolous claims. Axon Investigate is a good software for analyzing video sources. It allows detectives to play back video and determine if it has been altered. It also provides all the metadata, including where the video originated, date, time, frame rates, dropped frames, image numbers, and anything else you could want as a police agency. It also reduces the need for multiple proprietary systems to review video from different playback systems. Users can drag the footage into the program and allow it to do its thing. Best of all, agencies can create final analyses of videos that can be introduced into judicial settings.

Over the years, I have seen many cases where a cell phone video pops up on social media that appears to portray an agency in a bad light. While chiefs and sheriffs may turn to their bully pulpit to say that the video does not show the whole story, agencies are in a better position when armed with technological facts revealed by a video analyzer.

BLUEPRINT—CHAPTER 6

MOBILE VIDEO ON THE GO

1	What's your story and plan? Stick to it.
2	Place the phone in "Do Not Disturb" or "Airplane Mode" during filming.
3	Attach microphone and test audio.
4	Use a three-point lighting technique.
5	Focus the camera on the subject or talent (don't leave this to chance).
6	Use a stable platform (tripod or gimbal).
7	Use the rule of thirds in positioning the camera.
8	Press record.
9	Accumulate appropriate B-roll.
10	Use slow, steady pans.
11	Edit video.
12	Distribute videos across social networking sites.

VIDEO EQUIPMENT CHECKLIST

1. Smartphone, DSLR/mirrorless camera, or professional camcorder

2. Video lighting (portable; Lume Cube has great lights)

3. Microphone (DJI Mic compact digital wireless system works well or RØDE wireless)

4. Headphones (Sony MDR-7506 are inexpensive and work great)

5. Tripod (video with fluid head)

PRO TIPS

- Video outperforms other content types when it comes to brand awareness.

- Agencies can use visual storytelling to tell complex stories, highlight employees, and showcase the great work being accomplished.

- Your body camera and dashcam systems serve as an instant repository for compelling video sources.

- Video is an effective medium for teaching and sharing your brand with the community.

- Tools are available to assist the department when video is weaponized against the agency.

CHAPTER 7

AUDIO STORYTELLING

n August 2023, a shooting occurred in a quiet neighborhood that involved three armed suspects shooting at each other. Miraculously, no one was injured or killed. There was property damage to homes and cars. The incident sent shockwaves through the community. The gun violence captured by a doorbell camera was appalling to neighbors. Media attention was intense. Within a few days of the incident, our detectives had identified the main players and secured their arrests. This incident catalyzed a new podcast to educate the community on how the organization investigates gun crimes. It became a huge hit with thousands of downloads.

Audio is another tool for police agencies. Audiences go to different places to consume content. Some peruse social media feeds, others attend town hall meetings and events, some prefer videos, and some individuals prefer to listen to audio stories.

AUDIO STORYTELLING

Let's explore a form of communication that is seen less often in policing circles compared to video engagement—audio podcasts. The term "podcast" can be traced back to two creators who combined the words iPod and broadcast.[47] Since then, podcasts have increased in popularity and have especially gained prominence over the past decade. Before you nix the idea, see how easy it is to create a podcast and reach a high volume of community members.

Law enforcement agencies rarely utilize podcasts. While some departments have found success with podcasts, I think the reason it is underutilized compared to other social media is because of a lack of knowledge on how to structure podcasts, create content, and distribute shows.

WHAT IS PODCASTING?

A podcast is a tool to distribute audio content over the internet.[48] Consider current-day podcasts as on-demand media. A citizen can launch the podcast from many devices, including smartphones, and listen whenever desired. Unlike a rolling Facebook feed where a post from your agency may get buried after several hours or a few days, podcasts stay in the same order as they are released, meaning that a subscriber or community member who stumbles upon your podcast will always be able to easily access your published content.

Podcasts have been around for a long time. George W. Bush became the first US president to distribute a weekly podcast in 2005. While like a radio broadcast, the main difference is that podcasts are not aired live. Creators prerecord, edit, and upload content to a hosting service and platform.

Looking at data published in 2023, there were around three million active podcasts.[49] Nielsen published that 50 percent of all US homes are podcast fans, with an estimated 155 million Americans listening to podcasts.[50] The top two genres of podcasts include society and culture, counted as one category, and education, making up a combined 26 percent of the types of podcasts that people are listening to. Law enforcement agencies can be successful with podcasts, as listeners are drawn to crime stories and want to learn more about how police and sheriff departments operate.

STRUCTURE OF LAW ENFORCEMENT PODCASTS

An agency can create a show and publish various episodes. Each episode should follow a consistent structure, usually with a host or cohosts, and discuss relevant topics related to the criminal justice system and organization. Once the episode is ready for the world to hear, you distribute the podcast on the web via RSS so that listeners can find the show and access it through a listening app.

Apple Podcasts and Spotify are the two big players in the audio app world. Sorry for my fellow YouTubers, but YouTube is not a podcast medium. Yes, I know that many podcasters film their podcast operation to create videos and post them to YouTube; however, it is still considered a video search engine.

GETTING STARTED

Here are some basic steps to develop your show and get into a regular rhythm of producing and publishing episodes:

1. Define your strategy and goals.
   - Like any social media strategy, you must first ask yourself what purpose the podcast will serve.
   - Why do you want to start a podcast? Who is your audience? What podcasts already exist in your community? These questions will assist you in developing goals and thinking strategically about tapping into a new army of potential listeners. When I began the WSPD

Briefing Room podcast, our team determined early on that we wanted to increase transparency, elicit help on cold cases, and educate citizens on how we provide services to the community. From that basic template, we could innovate content that resonated with our listeners. Within weeks of our launch, we had developed a following of over three thousand regular listeners, which isn't bad for a town of under twenty thousand residents.

2. Establish your brand for the podcast.

- Start with potential names for the podcast. It should capture the essence of why people should listen. It should also be easily searchable across podcast directories. I have seen some catchy names that worked well for agencies. As for my team, we kept it simple—the WSPD Briefing Room. When creating a name, search and make sure that the name is not already taken. The name is important because podcasting services like Apple use the title as the basic form of their search engine. As you contemplate the brand, write out ten episodes that would benefit your agency so you know you're on the right track. If you can't think of ten, go back to the drawing board on the brand.

- Create artwork for your podcast. You can create this yourself or contract it out through a service like Fiverr. The artwork is very important! It is the first thing that potential listeners will see. In other words, it conveys to your audience why they should click on your podcast. There are some specific requirements to follow. Ensure you are creating the artwork (or contracting it out) to these specifications (e.g., square image 3000 x 3000 pixels, 72 dpi, PNG or JPEG, and color space RGB).

3. Choose your content style.

- Will you do interview-style podcasts? Will there be a cohost? Will the main host switch out from time to time? Will it be documentary-style? Will you do a hybrid approach where you may vary the content between documentary and interview styles? Will you disseminate events or news? Will this be purely educational in nature?

- Will you script or choose an impromptu style for your episodes? If scripting, you need to appear as if you are conversing versus reading.

- Determine the average length of your episodes. While each episode may vary in length, according to Buzzsprout, an optimal length is somewhere between twenty and forty minutes.[51]

- How frequently will you publish? Don't overcommit yourself, especially during the start. We all have very busy schedules and juggle many important tasks. When I first started, I challenged the team to try to publish two episodes a month with publication every other Friday morning. There is some strategy for keeping a consistent flow when episodes drop.

4. Get some recording equipment and editing software.

- You need a microphone, some headphones, and editing software at a minimum. Don't search for "podcast equipment" unless you have deep pockets. There are many other options to create good audio that won't upset your finance director.

- Dynamic mics work great for podcasts. While not getting too technical, a dynamic microphone picks up less background noise.

- Upon completing a recording, you need to edit. While some free options are on the market, there are also paid platforms. Apple's GarageBand is free. Audacity is free and also works on Windows computers. Adobe Audition is a paid software. Hindenburg PRO is also a paid platform. Do your homework and see what works best for you and your team.

- My go-to setup includes the RØDE RØDECaster Pro II (which makes recording a breeze), two RØDE PodMic dynamic broadcasting microphones, a foam windscreen for the mics, and two Sony MDR-7506 headphones. Why two? I like to do interviews, so having at least two is important. I use Hindenburg PRO software to edit the podcasts. That's it!

5. Establish a studio (or a quiet place where you can make some audio recordings).

- This location should be free of distractions and noises (police radio, telephone ringers, computer sounds). I have seen setups that are inside small rooms or even closets. Choose a location where the spoken word will not echo and come across as natural. Furniture, carpet, and curtains can help absorb sounds versus noise bouncing off hard floors and across open spaces.

- Position your host, along with anyone else who will be on the show, near the mics. Make a test run and check your audio levels. Plenty of instructional videos can show you how to do this.

- Start your podcast. Have fun with it! It's not live, so mistakes are fine and can be edited out later.

6. Embrace the world of editing.

- You need to create an engaging intro sound bite with music. While this can be accomplished in-house, I contracted mine out to a podcast developer on Fiverr. I had a professional intro and outro for less than a hundred dollars.

- Don't use copyrighted music. This is the fastest way to have your show removed from online. You can purchase rights to audio music and sounds through Storyblocks, Adobe, Soundstripe, and AudioJungle.

- Start your edits for content first. Get the flow down and ensure your story transitions from one topic or idea to another. Once the structured content is finalized, then go back and edit for distractions like unwanted noises and "ums."

- Listen to the finished project before exporting it to an audio file. If you subscribe to a podcast hosting service, such as Buzzsprout, they will automatically handle the proper format and add ID3 tags (metadata that enables your audience to find the show and episodes).

7. Determine a hosting service for your podcast.

- A podcast hosting service is a lifesaver for storing your show and episodes. It also handles the distribution of major podcast listening services for you.

- While there are many options out there, I have only used Buzzsprout. After I completed a few questions, Buzzsprout listed my show in all the major directories, enabling our audience to find our show.

8. Prepare for the formal launch of your show.

- As the big day nears and you have cleared all the hurdles—including being officially listed in the major directories like Apple Podcasts, Spotify, Google Podcasts, iHeart, and others—you are ready for the branding and marketing campaign.

- Start by releasing some teasers across your existing social media platforms. Don't discount a formal news release, either. Make a big splash on social media once you pick a date for the first episode. People will gradually find their way to your show over time.

- Stick to your strategy and goals. Most importantly, consistently record and publish your episodes to continually grow your followers.

SELECTING A HOST

In the podcast industry, a host should be a character in their own right.[52] It could be a strategic communication advisor or a leader. In my case, I lead most of the shows as it doesn't take a lot of effort to execute. Some agencies may use a recruiter, two hosts as a team, or pass the baton around the department and switch up the hosts. Think strategically about who has the capacity and can best connect with your audience.

FREQUENCY OF EPISODES

Don't overcommit. For most agencies, this means no more than two episodes a month. The shininess of the new podcast will wear off internally, but consistency will keep listeners subscribing and leaving positive reviews.

PODCASTS AS A COMMUNICATION TOOL

Some of your listeners will undoubtedly be new, meaning they don't already follow you on your social media feeds. This is what makes audio storytelling a great tool. You will reach people that you normally wouldn't. It's also a great opportunity to showcase different content that lends itself better to audio stories.

BLUEPRINT—CHAPTER 7

PODCAST EQUIPMENT

- RØDECaster Pro II two-person podcasting kit (comes with two mics and desktop stands)

- Sony MDR-7506 headphones (you need two)

- Buzzsprout podcast hosting service (online)

- Hindenburg PRO editing software

PRO TIPS

- Podcast checklist: script, prepare, record, edit, publish.

- Podcasts are great for recruiting, explaining processes, highlighting programs, cold cases, and documentaries.

- Audio storytelling allows communities to listen to content in their automobiles, anywhere on their smartphones, and in their homes.

- Audio programming allows agencies to show a creative side in connecting with the community.

- A small investment in audio equipment will ensure your audio storytelling comes across as professional.

- Have a strategy in choosing your topic areas for audio, much like you choose stories to tell on social media and through video.

CHAPTER 8

NAVIGATING CRISES AND CRITICAL INCIDENTS

During the summer of 2015, my department became embroiled in a controversial officer-involved shooting that would reignite protests in the Black Lives Matter movement nationwide. A call to a local car dealership about a suspicious person involved in a potential burglary ended with an officer-involved shooting. Almost a year to the day after the death of Michael Brown in an officer-involved shooting in Ferguson, Missouri, our incident had more unanswered questions than answers at the onset of the investigation.

The case became the latest in a string of unarmed Black men shot at the hands of police. This incident involved a young man named Christian Taylor. The narrative quickly spiraled out of control within a day of the incident. Not only did the story captivate the nation's interest, but the incident also went international. Checking email was virtually impossible, as the number of emails received from news organizations and citizens overwhelmed any ability to keep up. Every news station, internet blogger, and citizen journalist wanted interviews.

The most difficult part of trying to manage the incident was the lack of information from the involved officer about what had happened during the deadly force encounter. At the time, the involved officer did not make a statement for a couple of days. This case predated the proliferation of body cameras. Yes, there was some surveillance footage of certain aspects of the incident, however, there was no video of the actual confrontation and shooting. We only knew some "altercation" happened between the officer and Taylor. Vague language, without specific facts, was a characterization of an encounter rather than a detailed description of the actions of those involved.

Imagine trying to release limited information and using the term "altercation" without providing any further context or details. This allowed celebrities and citizens to fill in the information void and substitute any narrative. This is all we had to work with. Our agency was put through the wringer for the lack of information and the perception by some that the department was hiding facts. The relationships that we had before the incident were strained at best. Seeking to add credibility to the investigation in the public's eyes, the department invited the Federal Bureau of Investigation to participate in the review. It was all hands on deck, with the police chief and executive team reaching out to their circle of influence and discussing the need for calm while reassuring the community that a thorough and expedient investigation was underway. The department released audio of the 911 calls, police dispatch radio traffic, and created a dedicated webpage to house all the releasable information.

Even with the attempts to be transparent, the firestorm surrounding the shooting continued to grow. Rampant misinformation needed to be addressed. As soon as the officer's statement was received, the department acted. A scripted press conference that presented the facts was held. Focusing on healing through intentional listening sessions and community conversations gave citizens a voice. Within five days of the tragic incident, media headlines shifted more favorably toward the agency. Rumors diminished. As Dan Solomon wrote, "Transparency and action after an officer-involved shooting indicate a fundamental shift."[53] This incident transformed the way I approached and messaged crises.

CRISES AND CRITICAL INCIDENTS

Law enforcement is a business filled with risk, so crises and critical incidents will occur. Some crisis incidents will be portrayed negatively on social media. Some critical incidents will be subject to intense community questions. Some individuals may demand accountability without regard to the actual facts of the case. Other critical incidents will go largely unnoticed, especially if no controversy exists. And some will undoubtedly become front-page news and linger in news cycles for days or even weeks.

If I were asked to rate the importance of each chapter, managing a crisis would certainly rise to the top. When agencies encounter crises and critical incidents, they are at a crossroads that can lead to lasting ramifications for their organization and the law enforcement profession. At the proverbial fork in the road, there are two paths. One leads down a dark road with many pitfalls and problems. This path is fraught with stress and trouble. This path typically involves indecision, miscalculations, and improper, slow, or missing responses. As leaders and strategic communication advisors, we want to avoid this path.

While the second path is not the land of promise, it is the one we want to seek out as leaders. This path may contain issues, but it will lead us to the other side, where we can regroup and rebuild community trust following a crisis or restore order to a hurting community. This preferred path typically starts with a good command of the facts, a strategic assessment of the situation, and responsive and timely information releases.

Crisis and critical incident are terms that are routinely used interchangeably; however, they differ in meaning. Organizational critical incidents may include an officer-involved shooting, serious fleet crash, or line-of-duty death. External critical incidents may be an appalling crime spree, fatality crash, or other incidents that shock the conscious and are deemed newsworthy. While not every critical incident turns into a crisis, the approach to messaging has parallels.

A crisis is an incident that could overwhelm the agency and strain communication resources. Examples of organizational crises may be serious officer misconduct that becomes public, controversial use of force, or deadly force that appears illegitimate in the eyes of the community. External crises may include an active shooter incident, a school bus crash with children onboard, or an aircraft crash. Each crisis may have different information demands, community outcry, and response protocols.

No agency is immune from public and media scrutiny. There are no free passes. While rural and small-town America were rarely covered in the media just a few decades ago, the proliferation of social media, citizen journalists, and media connectivity have brought every agency into global media reach. Many agencies encountering a crisis are small, with no strategic communication advisor, no public information office, no team of communicators, and, often, with a leader who has never had any formal training or on-the-job experience dealing with a crisis. That's why leaders and advisors must create a crisis plan in advance for their agencies and train like their careers depend on it.

HOPE IS NOT A STRATEGY

Hoping to get through a crisis or incident is not a strategy. I've heard leaders say, "I hope our media strategy works," or "I hope the negative social media posts diminish," or "I hope the weekend gets here so people forget." Hope without specific actions is just that—hope. This is a fallacy where you relinquish control of the situation to the whims of information flows. It leads to reaction versus proactively addressing the incident.

The problem with this mindset is that you are saying you don't have a strategy. A strategy ensures that your team has goals and objectives, with intentional messaging directed at specific audiences tailored to each platform and channel. Leave hope out of it.

WHY TRAIN?

Training will assist an agency in preparing for a critical incident and crisis. Crises and critical incidents typically generate public questions and news stories. I like to remind leaders that the real definition of a major incident (crisis or critical) is an event that pulls the agency into the spotlight, requiring extensive organizational time and energy to navigate.

Your organization's reputation and image are on the line. This is why we must train. Agencies are only as good as they train. We need to host mock press conferences. We need to do tabletops on critical incidents. We need to evaluate our projected media strategy during training. We need to assess our communication tools along with messaging. Being strategic in communications requires a commitment to train regularly. Remember that your organization is best positioned to tell its own story. Adopt strategies during an incident using a fact-finding, fact-releasing methodology to empower the community, reaffirm the agency's competence to handle the situation, and move the narrative along. Lingering in an adverse news cycle with no end in sight is like operating a sailboat with no sail. Training determines how our teams will execute during a crisis or critical incident.

TOOLS

Don't be afraid to properly leverage all the tools in your toolbox to diagnose, respond to, and message during a crisis. The remainder of this chapter is broken down into five sections:

- Section 1: Before The Crisis—Preparation Stage
- Section 2: Crisis Identification—Assessment Stage
- Section 3: Immediate Action—Response Phase
- Section 4: Managing Crisis—Extended Phase
- Section 5: Demobilization Of Crisis—Recovery Phase

SECTION 1: BEFORE THE CRISIS—PREPARATION STAGE

1. Have a memo on how dispatch will notify you as a leader or strategic communication advisor that a major incident is happening.

2. Understand how your boss (or bosses) want to be notified. How will you communicate with them? When will you notify them?

3. Establish a master external contact list containing leaders/CEOs/communication professionals of major businesses, corporations, and venues in your jurisdiction. It's a good idea to host an annual luncheon with everyone to keep the list updated.

4. Have relationships with key community leaders—faith-based, social service organizations, civil rights groups, and others.

5. Train your organization on what to expect regarding communication during an incident.

6. Consider forming a community advisory board of key individuals to train on communication strategies, incident management, and other strategies (you are creating allies to stand with you during a crisis).

7. Create a strategic communication plan, a crisis communication plan, and a written media relations policy.

8. Train annually on the plans.

9. Visit newsrooms annually or host media mixers to maintain a positive relationship with news officials.

10. Build a proactive trust bank with your community through social media, videos, audio programming, publications, and other strategies to increase positive relationships and support with the community.

Preparation starts with a crisis communications plan and training. One could also argue that "prevention" of an organizational crisis should be included in the preparation phase. For example, suppose de-escalation training can prevent a use-of-force incident that could propel the agency into a crisis. In that case, prevention should be key in your strategy.

Any crisis has the potential to spiral out of control and strain relations between the police and the community. Many moving pieces will occur during an incident, requiring leaders to make various decisions. Don't underestimate the importance of the decisions related to communication. As the gatekeeper for authoritative information, the agency should be the initial voice on the crisis. Yes, I know many other decisions involving operations, investigative paths, and managing community relationships and bosses will be undertaken. The initial response, statement, and communication strategy will set the tone for how the incident plays out.

Your agency should be well-positioned regarding community trust before a crisis. Key relationships should already be established—having strong community support is crucial during a crisis.

Establishing a crisis plan to supplement your strategic communication plan is also a priority before a crisis occurs. The crisis plan sets the guiding principles to assist the agency in navigating the storm. When you are in the thick of it, it's difficult to remember all the items needed to manage the communications.

Along the line of the crisis plan, a critical incident checklist is extremely helpful. Leaders, communicators, and first-line supervisors can utilize it as a resource to ensure initial steps are completed from a communications perspective. Train on the checklist. Create scenarios that apply to your community. Review your crisis plan, once established, annually.

HOW DO YOU GET NOTIFIED?

Leaders and advisors need a way to receive notifications. In my tenure, we have used text messages to city-owned devices (not the most efficient manner) and relied on telephone calls. Upon my appointment as police chief, I adopted the platform Evertel, whose CEO is former Fort Worth Police Chief Jeff Halstead. Evertel has worked well for our dispatch to send command notifications through the mobile app based on a list of calls the executive team wants to be notified about.

CRISIS AND CRITICAL INCIDENT TRAJECTORY

Typically, a natural flow of events occurs during a crisis or critical incident. The incident occurs, officers respond, and it becomes classified as breaking news in the media. Investigators, other officials, and agencies arrive at the scene to assist with managing the situation. The community and media request information about what is happening and what they need to do.

Between the organizational response and community/media requests for information, a danger zone exists, creating an opportunity for misinformation to spiral out of control. When our agencies are not talking about the situation, other sources (citizens, pundits, so-called eyewitnesses, lookie-loos, and five-minute claim-to-fame individuals) will fill the void. It cannot be overstated that initial narratives become harder to change as the crisis evolves.

The next stage is public reaction after the agency provides information to the community and media. Does the community believe what you are saying? Do they think your agency has the capacity and competence to deal with the incident? Are they satisfied with the response? Is the community in shock? Your department must reevaluate or reaffirm the messaging strategy based on the public reaction.

At some point during the incident, the story will reach its peak. The news cycles will change, and the story will fade. It may completely die out and only resurface when again deemed newsworthy (i.e., court appearances, anniversaries, funerals, release of significant details not previously covered).

NEWS CYCLE DIAGRAM

Managing an incident's information flow correctly from the beginning is imperative. This will place the agency in the best position to deal with the crisis. The goal should be to guide the conversation, grounded in facts, to reduce the likelihood of misinformation. Being aware of the danger zone, the agency should strive to release vetted facts quickly to minimize false information from circulating in the community. As society is now more connected than ever, speed is of the essence.

CITIZEN JOURNALISTS

Remember that everyone in the community can become an instant "reporter" and start writing posts, calling friends, taking pictures, shooting videos, and notifying the media of their perspective. They often get the story wrong. Social media will start flaring up and can become unmanageable. The naysayers, robots, and trolls may see an opportunity to fan the flames. Unprepared organizations can be left with confusion and frustration. This is where a methodical and time-proven approach is required to manage a critical incident.

WITHDRAWALS FROM TRUST BANK

A crisis will affect your agency. I equate it to taking a withdrawal from your trust bank. Before the crisis, if your agency communicated strategically, you may have had a lot of trust in the bank. Your goal is to ensure that when something goes wrong, you still have enough trust in the back to cover the withdrawal. Once the crisis has been mitigated and dealt with, start making deposits again with great social media content, videos, and other ways.

SECTION 2: CRISIS IDENTIFICATION—ASSESSMENT STAGE

1. Once notified, consider possible approaches, develop an initial feel of the incident, and sift through the available information. Ensure someone on the scene, preferably in a command staff level position, updates information directly to you until your arrival.

2. Make your initial notifications to your boss (or bosses). Remind them that initial information is just that—initial, which can be incorrect.

3. Grab your emergency go kit (batteries, laptop, PIO vest, pen, and notepad). Bring your strategic communication and crisis plans, which will serve as the foundation for communication.

4. Respond to the scene and connect with the Incident Commander to start the strategic thinking using the ACE template—Assess, Choose, Execute, and Evaluate.

5. As part of the assessment, what are the safety and traffic impacts? Are there any hazardous materials or outages? What areas are affected? Does the public need to take any protective actions? Are there any public shelters? What about special needs populations (languages, disabilities, and Braille)?

6. Scan social media to see what's being said (or posted in a video).

7. Host a "circle assignment meeting or huddle" with the Incident Commander, investigative supervisor, detectives, and those responsible for communication. Make assignments as needed (see checklist for positions). Leverage the messaging triangle—community, employees, and bosses. Prepare actual sound bite and key messages through the FACTS method.

8. Messaging tone should follow the messaging cube: Authority, Balance, Call To Action, and Devotion.

9. Set a media staging area and notify media (blind copy email to news desks because if you publish on social media, nonmedia folks will show up).

10. Determine from the FACTS if there are any limits on releasing information (such as guilty knowledge).

11. Review (watch) relevant video involving the incident before making statements (body cameras, dashcams, surveillance footage, citizen-generated videos on social media).

12. Assess the level of incident or crisis. Do you need to establish a joint incident command with another agency or agencies? Do you need additional help? Some types of crises will typically require a quicker response compared to others.

13. Identify key stakeholders who will be important in your messaging. Who are your audiences? Are they civic organizations, civil rights groups, social service organizations, employees, or elected officials?

THE INITIAL NOTIFICATION

The clock starts once the initial notification of a crisis or critical incident is received. Executives need to orient their mindset to how the agency will respond. Pull out the crisis plan and critical incident checklist.

THE SPEED OF SOCIAL MEDIA

The speed at which information flows in the community is lightning-fast, based on digital engagement and social media. The speed at which vetted information flows back to leaders and advisors from the incident scene can be slow. This allows people to fill in the void with erroneous reports. Misinformation can be rampant, especially during the first few hours of an incident. The thirst for information from media, bosses, and the community can be overwhelming within the early stages of a crisis.

MAGNITUDE, TYPE, AND SCALING

There's no way to establish a comprehensive system of "if this happens, do that." Every incident is different. Incidents will require scaling based on changing dynamics and communication needs. Flexibility is necessary to scale up and down throughout an incident. If an agency deals with an active shooter with multiple casualties, the onset will require a high response to manage the narrative. As the situation stabilizes, the agency may be able to scale back some of its communication resources. Determining the proper need for resources during an incident is paramount to successfully managing the situation.

LEVELS OF CRISES

To assist executives and communicators, I developed a method to help agencies in their initial responses by assigning levels to incidents. Incidents can become crises due to community impacts, inappropriate operational handling, or improper or inadequate management of public information. During the initial notification and response, assign a level to the incident or crisis to help determine the proper communication approach and create a better organizational response.

- Level 1 Incident—This includes controversial officer-involved shootings, in-custody deaths, or uses of force (key word is controversial). It also includes allegations of officer inaction in stabilizing a scene, gross negligence by an officer through act or omission, serious or fatal crashes alleged to have been caused by an officer, serious misconduct allegations, and significant policy failures by the department that become public.

  Level 1 incidents threaten the organization's legitimacy, bring the department into disrepute, or cause (or are likely to cause) significant reputational damage to the agency's brand and image. They typically turn into a crisis.

  These types of incidents will necessitate an "all-hands-on-deck" approach. Contact peer agencies for communications support if you are a small to midsize agency. Respond to the scene and follow the checklist and methods in this book to stay in front of messaging and influence the narrative as the official source of information. Major executive organizations that support law enforcement leaders may also assist. Some agencies may even consider reaching out to a reputable consulting agency, depending on the magnitude of the crisis.

- Level 2 Incident—This includes an allegation of misconduct, incompetence, or vote of no confidence against the leader or senior command staff. Employees or outsiders could make the allegation. Also included in a level 2 incident could be organized efforts by labor groups to undermine the credibility and efficient operation of the department through work stoppages, vocal/written discontent with the agency, or a concerted effort to overthrow the administration via elected officials, senior city management, traditional media, or the community. Lawsuits targeting the agency that generates media attention would also be classified as level 2.

- Level 3 Incident—This is an incident or crime that shakes the perception of safety in the community and leads to a feeling of vulnerability. Also included are incidents that result in significant injuries or loss of life. Any incident covered extensively by the media or involving social media that could turn negative toward the agency would also be classified as a level 3 incident. These situations can easily transform into crises in various ways—an appearance of a lack of empathy by the agency, a perception the agency is adequately mitigating or investigating the crime, or erroneous narratives that are difficult for the agency to correct.

- Level 4 Incident—Includes an incident with a low probability of becoming a crisis. These types of situations, which may require a media response and community messaging, are considered routine in the natural workflow of a law enforcement agency. Examples include a homicide, a fatal crash, or a search for a serial robber.

- Level 5 Incident—This includes when an officer is killed or seriously injured due to the felonious actions of a suspect. It also includes officers wounded or killed in crashes or by suicide and unexpected deaths due to illness or health issues. While these are classified as level 5, this does not mean that they are less important than a level 1–4 crisis. By classifying as a level 5, agencies can approach these tragic incidents involving one of their own with the highest regard for honor and reverence.

  Level 5 incidents require more focus on internal messaging. Family considerations come first over public and media responses. A level 5 crisis will generate the same, if not more, media and public attention as other incidents, and rightly so. Level 5 incidents deserve the utmost attention.

> Messaging should not be published until family members have been notified. Other agencies should never break the news (for example, by posting a social media message with thoughts and prayers before a public announcement). Employees should receive information before the media and the public. In some cases, especially with deaths due to natural causes, there may not be a media release or public comments, depending on family wishes.

Awareness of the different incident levels is intended to frame the initial response. Any incident can become a crisis. The goal is not to be surprised. Being prepared by understanding the various levels will enable leaders and communication strategies to be more intentional, thereby increasing the probability of successfully mitigating incidents.

While incident levels 1, 2, and 3 should command the most immediate attention and messaging protocols, every agency should train across all levels and types of incidents to ensure their crisis plans are current. Execution of appropriate key messages at the right time to the right audiences is critical, regardless of the stage or level of an incident or crisis.

SECTION 3: IMMEDIATE ACTION—RESPONSE PHASE

1. Develop your crisis communications strategy (this includes your key messages and sound bites). Learn everything about the scene, players involved, location history, prior criminal history, contraband, weapons, and other pertinent information.

2. Determine if you need an initial holding statement or a full media brief.

3. Prepare by rehearsing with someone. Anticipate questions. Remember, "no comment" is not an answer.

4. Make an initial statement (in person and posted on social media) at the primary location. Avoid press conferences at multiple locations. The media staging area, with appropriate background, is a good press conference location.

5. The agency statement should be accurate, timely, and meet seven community information needs:

- Facts—What happened? What is the impact? What is being done about it?

- Call to action—What do we need for the public to do: shelter in place, leave the area, assist in locating someone?

- Magnitude—How big is the risk area? Am I affected? Is there a suspect at large? How much hazardous material has been released? How many people have been or will be affected? Will schools be affected?

- Immediacy—How soon will the community be affected? How soon will people need to do something? Where do we reunite with loved ones?

- Duration—How long will this incident last? When will people be able to go home? When will things return to normal?

- Competency—Who is in charge? Can they manage the incident? Can the issues be rectified? Can the problems be solved? Does the agency have the capacity to manage?

- Mitigation— Solve the crisis. Restore order. Restore faith in the agency. Unite the community. Demobilize and direct people back home. Complete the incident management.

6. Priority of Messaging—Early in the incident, health and safety considerations and impact on the community should be the priority of messaging. Later, the focus can shift to the actions to manage, investigate, and solve the crisis.

7. Key messages may include:

- The agency's dedication to resolving, mitigating, and investigating the incident and bringing those responsible to justice depending on the situation.

- Commitment to quick resolution and restoring order.

- Provision of resources that provide healing, comfort, and empowerment.

8. Facts should be released as they are confirmed (through social media, news releases, or at a press conference).

9. Don't forget to include information on what has been done to control the situation, mitigate the danger, and secure the area. How can the public stay informed (website, social media, community meetings)? Is there a hotline for tips? Include any public health concerns and traffic-related information (street closures, lockdowns, estimated reopening of roads).

10. Take questions and state you will try to obtain information regarding questions that could not yet be answered (within the limits of releasable information). It's OK to acknowledge that the requested information is not releasable at this time. Avoid hypothetical questions by answering, "It would be inappropriate for me to speculate on that at this time."

11. Don't arbitrarily set the next press conference time. Inform the media that a new time will be set once additional details are available.

FACTS METHOD

Use the FACTS method to remember key points when organizing your information to manage a crisis or incident. Forecasting allows chief executives and advisors to think strategically about what will be needed during the response phase during the incident. I refer to the first part of forecasting as the "initial feel" for the incident. As the first notifications come in, leaders will develop a general feel for the magnitude of the incident.

For example, I recall receiving notification of an incident where an officer shot at a dog charging toward him, and one of the projectiles fatally struck a woman. While driving to the scene, I initially felt this would become a crisis. Based on that assessment, our team developed an approach to messaging, which included consideration for the victim and the involved officer.

Assessment is continual throughout the incident, from initial notification to the final phase of demobilization. Judging the validity of information is paramount. While you are releasing information, you are also garnering additional assessments to assist with future messaging.

Coordination takes place during the circle assignment meeting or huddle, where information is obtained and decisions are made on what will be released. Coordination with other law enforcement entities, local school districts, or federal agencies may be required in large incidents.

Tell your story is where you communicate your key messages and sound bites to the public through the media. Telling your story is crucial during a critical incident.

Social media is used to reinforce the key messages that have been delivered to the media. Talk about the incident, highlight what is happening to manage the incident, and consider posting a video of your press event. Social media is an asset when responding to crises; the public will search official social media feeds during a critical incident, even before news breaks.

INITIAL HOLDING STATEMENT

In certain dynamic situations, time and information constraints may dictate that an agency release an initial holding statement and delay holding a formal press conference until more facts are known. The purpose of the holding statement is to release something from the official source (that's you) as soon as possible. A crisis plan should contain several preplanned holding statement templates for various situations. Here are the elements to include in a public safety holding statement:

- A factual headline that makes the type of incident readily apparent
- The date and time of the incident
- Location of the incident
- A vetted and confirmed sound bite or key message (This needs to be a basic fact statement)
- Any call to action, if needed
- An expression of empathy and compassion, if appropriate and supportive of the facts of the incident
- An anticipated media briefing time and location

Here's an example of a holding statement that might be used during a response to an active shooter: "On July 1, 2025, the Anytown Police Department responded to the 1500 block of Anytown Street in reference to multiple calls reporting shots were being fired. As officers arrived at the location, the officers reported multiple shots being fired. This is an emergency that is still unfolding with numerous officers at the location. As more facts become known, our police department will release information to the community. Those in the immediate area have been told to shelter in place at this time. Again, this is an emergency situation where police officers have the scene surrounded and are working to stabilize the scene. Our thoughts and prayers are with our first responders and those affected by this incident. We anticipate having a briefing at 4 p.m. at the media staging area."

CRISIS AND CRITICAL INCIDENT TRAPS TO AVOID

Many agencies fall into one of five traps during the initial stages of the incident. Agencies can remember these traps as SONAR.

- **S**peed
- **O**vercomplicating
- **N**onvetted facts
- **A**ccountability
- **R**eaffirmation

Remember, the goal is to inform and educate community members about what is happening. The first trap, *speed*, relates to agencies failing to get in front of incidents by taking too long to get initial information out. While law enforcement leaders know that initial information may be incorrect, basic facts can be readily apparent once some command and control have been established and the scene has been stabilized.

The second trap is *overcomplicating* the response. The KISS principle reigns true—using police jargon or not using logical statements that regular community members can understand will lead to misinformation or the appearance that the agency "knows more" than they are saying.

The third trap can result from releasing details too fast, leading to *unvetted facts*. Although acting too slowly is a trap, moving too fast, with a blatant disregard for basic facts, is detrimental. Agencies must find the sweet spot of getting to the scene, vetting facts, and making statements. Releasing incorrect, unvetted facts can hurt an agency's credibility. If an agency falls into this trap, incorrect information must be corrected quickly.

The fourth trap is creating a perception of a lack of *accountability*. People want to know what is happening and whether the law enforcement agency can handle the crisis or incident. Demonstrating accountability can take various forms but ensures community members have faith in the agency handling the situation. An agency with a huge trust bank can be better seen as competent in managing the scene.

The final trap is failing to engage in *reaffirmation*. In other words, agencies sometimes fail to reaffirm the vetted released facts. People's attention spans are short. Reaffirmation ensures that the agency's message is not only heard but is also reinforced. This is crucial when high-reach social media users are blasting the department with misinformation about a crisis or incident. Stick to the facts and reaffirm across your channels.

WHAT DOES MEDIA WANT DURING
A CRISIS AND CRITICAL INCIDENT?

The media wants access, professionalism, visuals, raw emotion from the scene, verification of facts from first responders, timely responses, and follow-up to unanswered questions. By having a plan to release factual information as it is confirmed, there is less likelihood for misinformation to develop and take hold. "A narrative is framed within the first few minutes of a crisis," according to Judy Pal.[54] Once a narrative starts to take shape, it is difficult to change.

Access requires allowing the media to access the scene so they can do their jobs. It also gives them access to public information officers, chief executives, and other officials who can provide appropriate information about the incident.

Professionalism is how we treat the media and community. Our job is to reassure the community, through our traditional media partners, that we are controlling and managing the incident. Professionalism is about setting up a staging area for reporters and giving them a reasonable timeline for a briefing. The relationships you have before the crisis are the same ones you will have during the crisis. Professionalism has to be the core tenet of how the agency manages information.

Visuals are what television and other media are going to capture during the incident. A good communications professional will consider in advance the types of visuals needed. Determine the best location for your briefing and control the background imagery.

Raw emotion from the scene is what reporters will be looking for. Incidents are dynamic and affect people's lives. The sense of urgency and police response are raw emotional elements of the scene. It is OK for chief executives to acknowledge terror, frustration, or other emotions that are part of the narrative.

Verification of facts is the most critical aspect of the initial communication. Organizations must release a basic fact set of what is known. This can be reinforced on the agency's social media channels. Provide the who, what, when, where, and how, in addition to the agency's plan for managing the incident.

Timely response to discuss the incident is critical. The media will find someone else to talk to if the agency isn't talking. Determine who will speak during the media briefing. Take questions.

Follow up with responses to unanswered questions at the appropriate time.

NATIONAL INCIDENT MANAGEMENT SYSTEM/INCIDENT COMMAND SYSTEM STRUCTURE

Leaders and advisors must have a basic understanding of the National Incident Management System (NIMS) and the Incident Command System (ICS) to enable effective and efficient incident management by integrating facilities, equipment, personnel, procedures, and communications operating within a common organizational structure.

The Incident Commander (IC) is responsible for the overall management of the incident. A Unified Command occurs when an incident affects multiple agencies or jurisdictions. Command Staff positions, including the PIO, may be established to assign/delegate responsibility for activities. The PIO is responsible for communicating with the media and coordinating with other agencies as necessary. Depending on the size or complexity of the incident, a lead PIO may have assistants, including support PIOs representing other responding agencies or jurisdictions. The PIO is a direct report to the IC.

JOINT INFORMATION SYSTEM
AND JOINT INFORMATION CENTER

The Joint Information System (JIS) integrates incident and event information with public affairs to provide consistent, coordinated, accurate, accessible, timely, and complete information during an incident. The Joint Information Center (JIC) is a central location that facilitates the operation of the JIS. It is a location where personnel perform critical communication tasks and crisis management.

I have established and participated in JICs for high-profile events and incidents such as the Super Bowl XLV, College Football Playoffs, natural disasters, fires, and child abductions. By having all the key communications personnel in one room, situational awareness, specific messaging, and overall strategy come together more efficiently.

SECTION 4: MANAGING CRISIS—EXTENDED PHASE

1. Some incidents require ongoing messaging. Multiple press conferences may be necessary. After each news conference, the lead communicator should reassess and gather additional details as they become known.

2. As the incident period evolves, changing the speaker may be required. For example, an active shooter incident may necessitate the community first hear from the police chief. As the situation evolves, other policymakers or political figures may be appropriate. Certainly, a level 3 crisis involving a line-of-duty death should have the agency's leader at the microphone. Rotate personnel assigned to communications as

    needed and watch for signs of fatigue and stress. Ensure all personnel are included in debriefs and peer support.

3. For longer-term incidents, consider providing power, restrooms, snacks, and drinks for news officials. You might need to consider long-term parking for satellite trucks if the news story goes national or international.

4. Press conferences may move to an indoor setting or your agency building.

5. Document the scene with photos and video from a communications perspective to share lessons learned in the future.

6. For certain crises, a dedicated website, also known as a dark website because it's invisible until deployed, may be necessary to communicate important information regarding the incident.

7. Exit the news cycle when appropriate. This can be accomplished with a final press conference. Certain crises that involve loss of life may generate additional news coverage as time pegs occur, such as memorials and funerals. Still, the incident should have finality with the public. The final press conference should include releasing relevant documents and digital media if authorized by jurisdictional statutes. Coordination with families, employees, and district attorneys should occur before release.

8. Determine if a critical incident video will be released.

9. Disseminate a news release to catalog the official statement of the incident.

OTHER ELEMENTS TO GUIDE THE NARRATIVE

"Feeding the beast" is a term describing the media's ongoing need for information from the agency managing the incident. In many cases, there will be multiple requests, sometimes even from the same outlet, for updates or additional facts surrounding the incident.

An example may be an incident involving the death of a child by an impaired driver. The emotional aspects of the story may generate additional news cycles and requests for information. Some elements that may assist include releasing certain 911 calls, dispatch audio, and jail booking photos.

While agency video or surveillance footage could also be released in some cases, a generally accepted view is to refrain from releasing items that may be viewed as insensitive or could cause additional emotional harm to the victim's family. Communicators can manage these requests with media outlets and explain their position of withholding (absent a FOIA request).

Caution should always be undertaken when releasing items of evidentiary value. In addition, some jurisdictions may have legal statutes that govern the release of media and information that pertain to the criminal investigation.

DUE PROCESS

Due process for involved employees in critical incident management is important for chief executives. Decisions and public information releases should not be made in a vacuum; a trusted confidant to bounce ideas off can help leaders ensure that messaging preserves due process.

Unless the crisis involves something so egregious that it shocks the conscience of the policing profession, it is best to reserve judgment during public comments and appeal for people to allow the investigation to run its prescribed course. A surefire way to lose employees is to cast negative judgment too soon in a use-of-force investigation. Have trusted advisors in the room with you to develop a communications strategy surrounding a controversial incident that involves an employee. The leader owns the decisions, including public comments, regardless of who makes the public release or what community members, bosses, or employees think. A solid foundation of community trust will buy an organization much-needed time in this scenario.

FINAL PRESS EVENT

There comes a time in the messaging cycle when a final press event should occur. If the goal is to eliminate an adverse news cycle, that might mean the next day. It boils down to the magnitude of the incident. An active shooter incident will likely remain in the news cycle for weeks. The goal of the final presser should be to release all available facts, materials, and other items that would close out the information side of the incident. If the media asks further questions in the coming days, the agency could return to the final press event.

DIGITAL MEDIA

There's an old saying that district attorneys run for election every few years, but chiefs run daily. As a leader, you own video releases from your dashcam and body camera systems. It's your call when and how to release, subject, of course, to public release laws in your jurisdiction. A district attorney might not like it, but it's your decision. If there is an incident causing so much community harm because citizens demand to see the video, it's a no-brainer—release it.

While each state has its own set of rules on releasing digital media, there has been a push in recent years to release video more quickly. Many leaders have seen firsthand the detrimental effects of sitting on video and being shown the door.

CRITICAL INCIDENT VIDEO

Many agencies are releasing their own critical incident videos, bypassing the media altogether, or disseminating the video to the media while posting it on social media. These videos typically incorporate some boilerplate legal language that reminds the community that the video is being released with the facts known at the time and that criminal and administrative investigations are still ongoing. A disclaimer warning sensitive viewers may also be included. Some of these videos are elaborate with a speaker, either the leader or strategic communication advisor, introducing the content of the video, followed by a graphics overlay of the incident scene. The critical incident video may include body camera, dashcam, and surveillance footage.

A frequent question arises regarding whether the agency should release all footage portions of relevant video surrounding the incident or make redactions. I will approach each of these individually.

1. Entire videos may be hours in length and involve dozens of officers. The media and public are interested in a video release's most compelling portions. As such, I do not release full videos of a critical incident.

2. Relevant video is best suited for critical incident videos. Relevant does not mean edited video. Relevant means an ordinary video length that led up to the encounter, shows the use of force, and closes with immediate aftercare or resolution. It can also include the relevant portion of the video at normal playback speed and then circling back to a freeze-frame, slow motion, or zoom.

3. Redacted video includes blurring items that are legally required to be redacted. Examples may be uninvolved people, children, and license plates. Also, agencies should uphold commonly accepted values of decency and refrain from showing points of impact from force or lifeless bodies. As determined by your jurisdictional laws, language by officers or the suspect may be kept intact or censored.

As a reminder, no videos should be released before officers provide compelled statements. In addition, no videos should be released without notifying involved officers and providing a copy of the intended release video to all employees before dissemination to the media or public.

In cases involving death during the use of force, a meeting with the family members of a decedent should be offered. A best practice is to offer to show them the relevant portions of a video before releasing it. These meetings with families should not include attorneys unless compelled by state law because the purpose is to notify them of the impending release and not to debate the case or discuss the status of the investigation.

Leaders should not be present in these meetings without a compelling reason. Remember, families of decedents will be emotional and hurting. Regardless of the facts of the case, this is someone's family member, so empathy and compassion will go a long way during these difficult situations.

EMPLOYEE LEAKS

Every agency deals with information leaks. The bigger the department, the more leaks. Don't be surprised if the media gets tipped off when one of your employees is arrested. I have even seen employees leak the names of officers killed in the line of duty before the agency made the official notification. While I will never agree with unofficial information leaks, it isn't easy to prove. As leaders and advisors, focus on what you can control—your official messaging.

BAD NEWS HAS A LIMITED SHELF LIFE

While the impact of bad news will lessen with time if properly managed, it might worsen if the agency does not deal with the incident from a messaging standpoint. One way to lessen the impact of bad news is to coordinate with other agencies. A leader may be "sitting on" some adverse news while waiting for the right time to dump it. If both agencies release negative news simultaneously, the stories may counter the news cycle to some degree. Approach this tactic with caution. Just because another agency releases negative information doesn't mean your bad news story is going away. And the media can often spot this tactic from a mile away.

THE POLITICS OF CRISIS

Depending on the incident, politics are sometimes inevitable. Corporations and businesses may have millions riding on public perception regarding their brands. Coordination and pre-established relationships can help navigate these situations, although, at the end of the day, the primary investigative agency owns the messaging. The agency should maintain objectivity to reduce perceptions that someone else controls or influences the narrative. The underlying goal for many cases where there is a high level of politics is to exit the news cycle as quickly as possible.

Here are three cases in point:

- In 2013, a woman plummeted to her death while riding a rollercoaster. Within minutes of the incident, social media was ablaze with people on the coaster tweeting about what they had just witnessed. Within an hour, the news reach was international. Close collaboration between public safety and the venue was critical. The tragedy was already horrific. There was no reason to inflame the situation further by having communication issues between the city and the venue.

- In 2021, a teenager was murdered outside an amusement park, steps away from the entry. The crime sent shockwaves through the community. Questions about safety were coming from every direction. Having a relationship with the park's public relations personnel greatly assisted with handling the incident. While politics did creep up in some behind-the-scenes conversations, the teams could work together to manage the outcome.

- In 2022, a military jet went down with the pilot safely ejecting. The incident became worldwide news within the first hour following the mishap. Key relationships established before the incident helped navigate the bureaucratic communication issues that arose in the initial stages of the incident, such as who would speak, what would be said, and how the investigation would proceed.

SECTION 5: DEMOBILIZATION OF CRISIS—RECOVERY PHASE

1. Recover your equipment and demobilize the operation at the scene.
2. Debrief your personnel and allow for a constructive critique of the communication strategy.
3. Allow for peer support needs, as necessary.
4. Participate in agency after-action reviews (these are not just for operational aspects; communications should be included).
5. Download news coverage of interviews and mentions of the incident.
6. Return social media to match your strategic communication plan.
7. Make updates to the crisis plan, if needed, based on the experience of this incident.

The goal in any crisis, whether organizational or community-based, is to restore a sense of normalcy and order. That means different things depending on the type of incident. As the active shooter incident unfolded in Allen, Texas, in 2023, an underlying communication goal was to restore a sense of safety to the community while honoring the first responders and victims involved in the tragedy. An officer misconduct scandal that rocks a department would have a communication goal of isolating the incident and restoring confidence in the department's ability to provide public safety services by highlighting the misconduct as not reflective of the entire organization.

Demobilization occurs after the management of the crisis. Your people will slowly return to normal operations. Take care of your communication personnel. As a leader, make time to debrief with the communications team.

MEDIA MONITORING

Safeguard footage for the case file. Many prosecutors have asked for news coverage of an incident during trials. It's also a way to critique your appearance and delivery during press conferences.

SERIOUS INJURY OR LINE-OF-DUTY DEATH

There will be certain incidents that require special handling. One of the most challenging situations arises when an agency experiences a serious injury or line-of-duty death. While extreme care should be maintained throughout the management of these types of incidents, confidentiality is critical during the initial stages of a traumatic event involving an employee. Regardless of agency size, executives and advisors should assume that the employee's identity and the nature of the injuries will be released through unofficial means (employee leaks). Be thinking of how to message your employees while balancing the needs of taking care of the immediate family. No details should be released before getting an immediate family member to the hospital.

There will be an emotional impact on the agency. This requires careful coordination of information. A designated location for grieving should be established. Plan on media showing up at the hospital. Make contact with the public affairs person assigned to the hospital with a reminder not to comment until messaging is coordinated with the agency.

In some cases, especially in dynamic law enforcement

situations, the incident may unfold with no apparent resolution suitable for the agency to release. Multiple scenes may also be managed, including a primary news conference location. Even if news media resort to team coverage at multiple locations, conducting official news conferences at one designated location is highly advised.

No information should be released until the following questions have been thoroughly answered:

- Has the immediate family (spouse, parents, adult children, or other loved ones) been notified of the incident and the employee's status?

- Have family members had an opportunity to be escorted to the medical treatment facility?

- Have internal employees been notified of the basic facts and status of the employee?

- Have senior organization leaders, such as the city manager, mayor, council members, and other important stakeholders, been notified?

Once initial notifications have been made, a media strategy should be developed. It may be appropriate to have the treating physician available for the press conference. News that may be emotionally difficult to deliver should be released with care. The leader, not the PIO, should always announce news related to a line-of-duty death. These are times when employees and the public need to hear from who is in charge.

A well-spoken and sincere message from the leader can go a long way in the eventual healing. It is a good idea to script a few bullet points to ensure the agency head stays on message and delivers the appropriate information to the community.

In cases involving death or serious injury, care should be taken when referencing the name and other identifying aspects of the family involved. From a best practices standpoint, the immediate family, through a designated person, should have a say on whether to release the officer's identity along with other family remarks.

APOLOGIES

In some cases, it is fine to offer an apology. A case in point involved a traffic stop of a family traveling to a sporting event. The initial stop was because the officer believed the vehicle was possibly stolen. An error was made because the officer ran the wrong state on the license plate. Moments later, the family was ordered out of their car at gunpoint. Once the mistake was discovered, the officers and supervisor at the scene apologized. Unfortunately, the on-scene apology did not prevent a national news story.

The police chief publicly apologized and committed to full transparency and a complete review to prevent future incidents. I applaud the speed and commitment of this agency to get in front of the story. Did it stop the news from running? No. But it did provide a perspective that communities could understand.

Don't apologize for incidents where the agency didn't do anything wrong. An apology when your team messes up is appropriate and may resonate with your audience.

CHECKLIST

One of my most requested items is a checklist I produced for the Police Executive Research Forum. Agencies nationwide have found value in it when faced with a dynamic and extraordinarily difficult crisis or incident. The checklist is easy to follow and has several addenda tailored to the type of incident.

The checklist is available for download at: www.policepio.com.

BLUEPRINT—CHAPTER 8

CRITICAL INCIDENT/CRISIS CHECKLIST

Section 1—Incident Information
Section 2—NIMS/ICS Structure
Section 3—Incident Phases | Assignments | JIS | JIC
Section 4—Public Information Needs During An Incident
Section 5—Priority Of Messaging—Sound Bite(s)—Key Messages
Section 6—Emergency Public Information Checklist
Section 7—Final Press Conference Considerations
Section 8—Officer-Involved Shooting/Deadly Force Encounters Addendum
Section 9—Line Of Duty Death/Employee Serious Injury Addendum
Section 10—Strategies To Deal With Adverse News Cycles
Section 11—Interview Strategies | Opening Statements | Anticipated Questions
Section 12—Press Conference Checklist
Section 13—Emergency Public Information Team Roles
Section 14—The Art Of Strategic Communication Diagrams

PRO TIPS

- As a leader, own your crisis. This means your agency should quickly release official, vetted facts about the incident and how the team manages it.

- The person in charge of communications must respond to the scene to obtain a full briefing of the incident.

- Never make a statement about an officer's actions before reviewing digital media.

- Develop your key messages and sound bite(s) using the FACTS method and messaging cube. Ensure you completely understand the facts. Consult your crisis plan for messaging templates.

- Reinforce your crisis communications through social media channels, websites, and notification systems.

- Incident awareness will spread quickly across social media. It's imperative that the organization talks about known facts in a proactive manner; otherwise, the agency will be in a response mode the entire time.

- Critical incidents make national and international news quickly. You don't have the luxury of playing ostrich and sticking your head in the sand.

- Don't let other agencies break your news—have conversations on the front end with your peers so they respect your timelines should the unthinkable happen to one of your employees.

- Disseminate information at one primary location, typically at a hospital, if available, versus the actual scene.

- Have a good relationship and develop rapport with medical staff, including their spokespeople, who can assist with managing media, offering briefing locations, and providing secondary speakers on medical prognosis or services rendered.

CHAPTER 9

WINNING NARRATIVES AND SOUND BITES

n 2017, during one of the busiest shopping days, mass panic erupted at a local mall. At the culmination of the Thanksgiving weekend, gunshots rang out in the mall's center near a food court. Within minutes of the incident, social media was abuzz with reports of an active shooter. National news outlets pivoted to breaking news alerts about an active shooter situation. Local stations were heading to the scene.

As responding officers and supervisors tried to get a handle on the situation, information began to emerge that this was an officer-involved shooting in the crowded mall. Being at a nearby event, I arrived quickly. Gathering the facts and trusting the initial vetting by the commander, I could correct the information about what was going on. It was not an active shooter but rather a shooting. Did that matter much to those frightened and affected by the incident? No. However, it did cool the media temperature down and reduce panic.

Conducting a quick scan of social media, the team observed a lot of rumors and outright lies. Posts erroneously claimed the suspect had had his hands up when the officer shot him. This continued to drive negative emotions as the incident unfolded.

During the early stages of the case, we determined that the gun the suspect had pointed at the officer trying to detain him for stealing some sunglasses was fake. It was essentially a BB gun. To prevent future issues, I decided to acknowledge the type of gun the suspect had in his possession. Again, the social media onslaught tilted negative. People could not understand that a fake gun would warrant the same deadly force response as pointing a real gun at a police officer.

With all the misinformation and Monday morning quarterbacking on why an officer would shoot a person pointing a fake gun, the sound bite had to speak to that issue. In front of the cameras, I reminded the community, "There's no training in the world that exists that I'm aware of where an officer would be able to, in a matter of seconds, readily distinguish between a real or a fake gun." That sound bite nailed it. Immediately, the narrative shifted, as people could relate to that statement. It made sense if someone was pointing a fake gun at a citizen, they would likely respond similarly—what we say matters.

WINNING NARRATIVES AND SOUND BITES

No one likes to endure negative social media or news stories. It's a double whammy when an adverse social media storm becomes a news story. Unfortunately, people comment on and share bad news. During an adverse story, remind yourself and the agency that this, too, shall pass.

Leaders also need to know that negative stories may seem more impactful than they are. If our leadership team is upset about a negative social media post or news story, I consult my "family/friend barometer." I call my family and friends and ask if they have even heard of what's going on. If the answer is no, my next call is to a trusted advisor at a neighboring police department. If the answer is still no, we may be overreacting inside the agency, and the news may not be as impactful as our team is making it out to be. Assess a story's true impact to guide your response.

Some stories are indeed so bad that they linger for a long time. This is where resiliency and peers come in. I have never had a leader or peer who did not offer support and encouragement when I was in the middle of a mess. Having someone to lean on can benefit your emotional health and may even lead to coming up with a strategy you hadn't thought of.

CONTROL

Let's start with this central tenet: you do not control how "they" tell your story. "They" refers to the media, community, and employees. There are countless examples where an incident unfolds, and the narrative quickly escapes from an agency. Often, this can be attributed to the agency being too slow in releasing information or people questioning the agency's response or perceived inaction. In this sense, you do not have control but can influence outcomes. Take, for example, the horrific and devastating wildfires that affected Maui in 2023.

Within a few days of Lahaina being destroyed, stories of communication failures with the County of Maui began surfacing. The narrative quickly shifted from the rising death toll to a critique of the failure to activate emergency sirens. People reported an overreliance on Facebook and other electric emergency alert techniques in an area with limited to no cell phone service and major power outages. The control of the narrative was in the hands of others, which is a precarious situation for any public safety executive to find themselves in.

FOCUSING ON WINNING NARRATIVES

A winning narrative is well received by the community, regardless of the incident, crisis, or situation. A winning narrative also resonates with the public. To resonate with someone through communication means to connect emotionally with them. The result is that the agency builds trust, rapport, and empathy through the narrative.

Winning doesn't always mean positive news. Winning means thinking and communicating strategically, during good and bad stories, to resolve, mitigate, and restore the public to preincident or precrisis standing.

This becomes important during situations that bring about controversy. Here's a real-life example. In 2012, an international headline ran, "Shocking video shows police officer body slamming girl, 15, to the ground during a street fight." As luck would have it, they were talking about my agency, and I happened to be tasked with reviewing the facts and providing a response. The video wasn't pretty, as most force is not. We drilled down to what had happened: the officer had used a straight-arm bar takedown tactic to control an unruly teen and prevent further physical violence. How could I create messaging that would form a winning narrative?

For starters, we slowed the video down frame by frame. We matched the video to the officer's statement. Our team determined the force used was reasonable based on the level of resistance. Now, it was my turn to address the media and the public.

From a winning narrative perspective, we laid the facts out. We shifted the conversation to our administrative force review process, which reinforced trust in the multilayer review that the community expects. We discussed the root issue of disobeying police officers attempting to de-escalate the situation. We appealed for calm with a call to action of not making rash judgments based upon a limited cell phone video that did not show the moments leading up to the encounter. That's all it took to bring the community temperature down through the media. A winning narrative succeeded.

FOCUSING ON SOUND BITES

A good sound bite captures the most important aspects of the narrative and summarizes information to influence the audience. It is not a dissertation. Keep a sound bite short, concise, and to the point. It takes work to develop good sound bites. One way to develop the skill is to incorporate them into your visual and audio storytelling and social media posts.

According to speechwriter Jeff Shesol, like a smoke ring, a sound bite is "a neat trick, maybe, but it's gone in an instant; it dissolves in the air."[55] Craig Fehrman said, "the average TV sound bite has dropped to a tick under eight seconds," compared to the 1960s when a forty-second sound bite was the norm.[56]

When you provide an interview to the media, they will likely grab a snippet and air it in only a few seconds. It's imperative to master a sound bite that will maximize the reach and influence of the story. Visualize the smoke ring evaporating almost instantaneously. Keep your sound bites brief and focused on the message.

STEPS FOR A WINNING NARRATIVE AND GREAT SOUND BITES

Start by creating an outline for the story. What elements are necessary to convey the story? What are your key messages? Which key message aligns with a sound bite? Isolate the sound bite and see if it stands on its own merit. Does the sound bite project trust, competence, and ability to manage, as applicable?

With a little practice, you can master a sound bite. With a great sound bite, key messages, and incorporating the four elements in the messaging cube, you will be cranking out winning narratives, even in tough situations.

MILITARY BLUF FRAMEWORK FOR
WINNING NARRATIVES (INTERNAL OR EXTERNAL)

In 2016, Kevin Kolbye, former assistant special agent in charge at the Dallas FBI Field Office and Arlington assistant police chief, introduced me to the BLUF framework—bottom line up front. BLUF communication places the essential information at the story's beginning. It is similar to an elevator speech, summarizing the main points in less than thirty seconds.

BLUF has origins in the US military. Like not burying the lede, audiences appreciate the main points upfront. Adhere to the BLUF technique to share the most vital information, coupled with the call to action, from the very onset of the conversation. This will assist with creating winning narratives and meaningful sound bites. Incorporate the BLUF framework for internal memorandums, emails, and community publications to increase readability.

RELATIONAL POLICING

Art Acevedo, former president of the Major Cities Chiefs Association who has held top posts in Austin, Houston, Miami, and Aurora, put the term "relational policing" on the map. "Relational policing is about a mindset. It's about an attitude, and it's about a spirit of service. It starts with the realization that any human interaction is the beginning of a relationship."[57] Rooted in principles of transparency, respect, engagement, emotional capital, accountability, and trust, relational policing provides opportunities to forge a positive relationship. This is achieved through in-person interactions, social media, town halls, and video engagement.

Many of the tenets throughout this book are also grounded on relational policing principles. Treating people respectfully, being transparent, and committing to citizen engagement increase accountability and trust. Internal messaging can infuse positivity into officer mindsets to align with these principles.

BLUEPRINT—CHAPTER 9

PRO TIPS

- Don't be afraid to connect with peers to strategize and create winning narratives.

- Agencies have no control over how "they" tell your story. Agencies do, however, influence appropriate messaging.

- Winning narratives orient the organization to the successful resolution of issues and problems.

- A sound bite is a snippet of a few seconds that might grab an audience's interest and attention and convey the story.

- Create compelling sound bites by assessing situations, targeting the audience, and crafting a message that is easy to understand and speaks to the situation.

- Bottom line up front (BLUF) writing styles enhance communication processes.

- Relational policing initiatives should be discussed with employees and highlighted on social media to build greater trust throughout the community.

CHAPTER 10

INTERNAL COMMUNICATIONS

n 2019, I responded to the dreaded call of an officer down. The veteran officer had been shot and transported to a local hospital. Details were sketchy, and his condition was not readily apparent. The scene was chaotic, with a hostile crowd developing. The shooting suspect had been shot and killed by a backup officer.

As I arrived, the incident commander provided the known facts. I reviewed digital media consisting of dashcam and body camera footage. I glanced at social media and saw some negative posts with misinformation. I told my boss, who was at the hospital with the injured officer, what I planned to say. After getting the green light, I prepared an email communication for the entire workforce, our city manager, and elected officials.

The purpose of the email was to focus on internal communication first. Once it was sent, we waited about a half hour before I spoke with the media, which gave me time to run through my narrative, key messages, and sound bite. I was also able to anticipate questions.

Internal communications can make or break a leader. This chapter analyzes some best practices to keep the workforce engaged with high satisfaction levels.

INTERNAL COMMUNICATIONS

Keeping up with internal communications can be overwhelming and daunting at times. Everything competes for your time and attention as a leader. Executives must not discount the importance of internal communications. One of the recurring themes from surveys of law enforcement officers is that internal communications continue to present challenges. A recent poll found three overriding issues cited by employees when asked what they wanted in their police agencies. They wanted agencies to care, to be consistent, and to communicate better. One can draw a parallel that employees believe executives do not communicate, appear inconsistent, and do not care.[58] Poor communication between people, functions, and departments bogs things down and keeps people from performing and innovating at a high level.[59]

These issues can be managed with proper attention to internal communications. Police officers and professional staff desire access to information, prefer consistency across various agency functions and want to work for a department that cares about its employees. When executives place value on the importance of internal communications, they send the message that access to information is central to the proper functioning of the department. It also enhances recruiting and retention and conveys that the organization is supported from the top down.

LEADER'S RESPONSIBILITY

Recurring and consistent communication from the agency head should be a priority. Agencies should also look at different ways to communicate. Consider electronic means, in-person activities, and technological solutions to communicate with employees.

EMAIL

While email is a quick way to disseminate information, it can be overused or used as an improper tool to connect with employees. In some cases, it can be difficult to determine tone. If email is used, look for strategic ways to create an electronic newsletter, coupled with images and videos, to assist in telling your story. As agencies continue hiring millennials and a younger generation workforce, email can feel like an archaic communication method. Some universities have found email so passé that they discontinued issuing email accounts. In addition, proper email etiquette and training may be necessary. For example, how to use the "to" and "cc" fields may warrant further discussion.

Leaders should remind employees that email is not a notification. In other words, it can be difficult, if not impossible, to read, digest, and respond to every single email. The takeaway is that if it's an important notification, pick up the phone and call or text—and if you text, ensure you receive an acknowledgment before assuming the message was received.

MOBILE APPS

One tool in lieu of email is an internal mobile app. Evertel is one that complies with retention laws and affords several advantages for internal communications. It can also be used as an alert and notification system for employees.

CONVERSATIONAL COMMUNICATIONS

Internal communications can also include in-person meetings, briefings, and informal water cooler conversations. Most executives know that employees may be reluctant to share important information, so repeated attempts and forums should be a focal point for agency heads. Create an environment demonstrating that you truly care for the team as a leader. Yes, what you say matters, so you must manage impromptu conversations to avoid the dilemma of someone claiming the "chief said" [insert whatever a person might claim the leader said].

EMPLOYEE GROUP MEETINGS

Meeting with employee groups and labor organizations should also be a priority. Set a recurring meeting, possibly quarterly or more often, depending on the level of topics. This ensures good communication between rank-and-file groups or associations and the leader's office.

INTERNAL APPOINTEE GROUPS

I appointed a formal group of employees representing each segment of the organization to meet quarterly and bring up issues while also dispelling rumors and disseminating important information. We called this group the shared leadership team. Many leaders have similar groups, such as a chief's advisory council or quarterly working group. The purpose is to create an additional pipeline of advocates armed with the most current information. As a leader, I would run proposed policy changes through the shared leadership team to receive feedback on how the changes would affect various department divisions and create greater buy-in. These groups can be appointed and serve predefined terms.

SKIP-LEVEL MEETINGS

Depending on the size and structure of your agency, a leader might consider hosting skip-level meetings with certain ranks. For example, I meet bimonthly with corporals and sergeants without their lieutenants present. This is not intended to keep information from the lieutenants; rather, it's an opportunity to grasp the issues and understand operations from the employees' perspective. During these meetings, a leader must set ground rules to ensure conversations aren't negative or overly critical toward other ranks or command staff. The leader also must demonstrate their resolve to preserve the integrity of the chain of command.

CHIEF'S OR SHERIFF'S BRIEF

One of the regular communication products that I have seen be successful is a weekly digital newsletter. In my previous agency, we called it the weekly *Wrap Sheet*. In my current agency, it's called the *Chief's Brief.* Irrespective of the name, the goal is to pack useful information from the past week, highlight great work, and forecast future events. Tailored for employees with short attention spans, keep these one page or less. They should also be easy to replicate from one week to the next. Regardless of their size, any agency can find a few items each week to highlight. We would disseminate on Fridays with a positive tone and content.

FORMAL AWARDS

Even a five-member department should have a formal awards program. Make recognition a priority and host an annual ceremony. Invite public leaders and other internal departments to attend. Make this a special event to highlight the great work of your teams.

In all my years in policing, donors have funded our awards ceremonies. This included catered food, door prizes, and the awards themselves. Punch out a letter to area businesses and ask for donations to host a ceremony, and they might donate.

Lifesaving awards or acts of bravery could even be highlighted at your public meetings. I often bring my officers to our city council meetings to publicly recognize them in front of the community. Plus, elected officials love seeing the cops and firefighters receiving formal awards.

COMMUNICATION CONTENT

Many executives ask what types of communication they should be conveying regularly. Each individual agency determines the answer to that question. A good rule of thumb is recognizing good performance, highlighting important announcements, and briefing employees on departmental business activities, such as city council meetings where law enforcement agenda items are discussed. The more information employees can access, the better off the agency is from the standpoint of being well-informed, reducing rumors, and correcting misinformation. Include items of interest that every employee, both sworn and professional staff, can find of value.

PRAISE IN PUBLIC—PRAISE IN WRITING

Early in my career, I worked for an agency that would publish disciplinary actions in a memorandum to the entire organization. While this was aimed not only to deter others from engaging in similar behaviors but also to eliminate rumors, the opposite occurred. The talk of the department centered on these memos and also caused the involved employee to relive the incident versus moving forward.

As executives and strategic communication advisors, we need to change the mantra of catching employees when they do something wrong to seeing employees when they do something great. We must focus on the positives and ensure that work that goes above and beyond is recognized publicly, appropriately, and in writing. If the head of the agency focuses on good, this mindset will start to permeate all levels of the organization. Before long, you will have an army of supervisors and frontline employees reporting positive workplace behaviors and great deeds. This type of leadership philosophy is contagious; the more you recognize employees publicly, the more good work will follow.

LISTENING PRINCIPLES

You probably have heard of the "80-20 principle," which comes from the world of sales and means that we should spend 80 percent of our time listening and just 20 percent talking.[60] What we learn through active listening can be used to connect with an employee. Avoid looking at your phone and make good eye contact. Consider open-ended questions to address any issues that are raised. This is an important form of internal communication whether people are in your office speaking to you or commanders are attending your meetings.

While we train our people in verbal de-escalation techniques to deal with the community outside our buildings, internal communication can also de-escalate employees' internal concerns. For example, an officer may be raising an issue from their vantage point that the administration has not considered regarding a policy change.

ROLL CALL SCROLLS AND DIGITAL DASHBOARDS

Important information, vacation watches, and bulletins can scroll on a television or computer screen as an additional communication tool.

Dashboards may contain officer activity training materials, celebrate life events (birthdays, milestones, personal achievements, and work anniversaries), display awards, and recognize officers' actions. First Arriving is one company that provides several dashboard configurations.

CRIME MEETINGS

Meet regularly regarding crime statistics and trends, problem locations, and intelligence. Invite officers to attend and send out a recap afterward.

CULTURE AND THE END GOAL
OF INTERNAL COMMUNICATIONS

Communicating well enables leaders to motivate, develop, and inspire employees to improve their jobs, resulting in healthier workplaces and strong communities. In pursuit of this end goal of internal communications, the IACP published a guiding document on ways to support positive cultural change.[61] It takes time to affect meaningful change, often years. The following strategies are outlined to enhance positive internal culture:

1. Identify goals and share vision: regularly communicate critical agency goals and needs through internal communication channels.

2. Be honest and transparent: be authentic and timely with communication.

3. Use emotional intelligence: A leader's attitude and tone can be contagious to agency members. Use it wisely.

4. Actively listen: learn to fully concentrate and paraphrase to demonstrate an understanding of the speaker's meaning.

5. Give credit: celebrate successes by publicly and privately praising employees' work. When everything is going well, the agency gets the credit. It lands on the leader's shoulders when everything is not going well.

6. Mentor: mentoring others to share the mission, vision, values, and goals will lead to a more effective organization.

7. Communicate in various ways: email, phone calls, video conferencing, face-to-face contact, mobile apps, and in-person meetings.

BLUEPRINT—CHAPTER 10

FIVE GOLDEN RULES OF LEADERSHIP

RULE #1—Don't bad-mouth your boss or peers.

RULE #2—Pay attention to your email and written communications, especially when upset. It's difficult to recover from something sent out in anger ("recall email" buttons rarely work).

RULE #3—Don't let employees enter your office and trash other agency supervisors, commanders, or executives. If there is an issue, professional and appropriate ways exist to handle it. Allowing them to "vent" by criticizing is dangerous and sets the tone for unacceptable behavior. If you allow this to occur, the next person they vent about could be you.

RULE #4—Leaders don't point out problems without providing solutions. When they solve issues, leaders reaffirm that the agency will be OK.

RULE #5—Don't let others steal your joy as a leader. Problems are everywhere; as one fire is extinguished, another one will pop up. Keep your positivity in place and project calm in the face of adversity.

BLUEPRINT: WAYS TO MOTIVATE WORKFORCE THROUGH COMMUNICATION

- Ask your supervisors and commanders if people follow them because of their authority or leadership style. If it's the latter, they are setting a good example by motivating their teams.

- Do you model a good example for your subordinates and employees as a leader through verbal, nonverbal, and written communication?

- Commit to lifelong learning through personal and professional growth opportunities. Challenge employees to do the same to better themselves and their teams through regular briefings, training, and workplace discussions.

- Invite employees to suggest policy changes when the written word becomes inconsistent with practices.

- Advocate for your people through recognition, praise, and highlights on social media.

- Ensure supervisors conduct appropriate briefings and reinforce communication from upper levels and the leader's office.

- Start your executive command staff meetings with praise, great work, and positivity.

- Build a professional internal network so communications continue while the boss is away.

- Gossip is bad for workplaces and can lead to major issues. Enact zero-tolerance policies on workplace gossip and ensure supervisors shut down gossip by leading by example, redirecting conversations to appropriate topics, and admonishing offenders that gossip is not allowed.

- A leader who communicates with facts and utilizes multiple streams for internal communications reduces the impact of any workplace gossip.

- Recognize good performance by reading commendations at roll call (not just sticking them into an employee's box).

- Instill a solution-focused leadership philosophy (leaders who solve problems) versus blame-based (managers who care more about things than people).

- The order of priority in communication is people, property, and policy. When getting bad news, the first question should be, "Is everyone OK?" Use "we" and "us" to convey partnership; "you" and "I" can create separation.

CHAPTER 11

BLOGS, AGENCY APPS, REPORTS AND PUBLICATIONS, AND WEBSITES

This chapter focuses on communication channels that are neither traditional media nor social media. Even if your social media team is setting records with community conversations, don't overlook the power of engagement via blogs, agency mobile applications, reports, other publications, and websites. These tools can be used to maximize reach and influence through credibility and visibility.

Law enforcement agencies produce a lot of paperwork. In my experience, many of the reports we prepare are not used. Reports, periodicals, newsletters, brochures, and other publications build credibility only if people can get to them.

Once the products are produced, visibility occurs through placement. Publications can be prominently displayed on your website, via social media, in an agency app, emailed to a distribution list, or placed as printed copies in a lobby.

Educational and informational materials validate the agency's professionalism. They make the agency credible; the organization is the official source of facts. Credibility and visibility produce positive momentum. More web clicks, app downloads, podcast views, video subscribers, and comments grow your followers and audience. Everything builds on each other. With a multifaceted distribution approach, these products enhance social media and visual or audio storytelling.

BLOGS

Blogs are unconventional ways to connect with communities. They are similar to social media but have different structure. Blogs are considered long-form content and can dive deeply into issues. They are in written form and sometimes include photos and videos.

For example, Kristin Lowman, assistant director for the Police Media Relations Office of the Dallas Police Department, uses storytelling via blogging in addition to publishing official news releases. This has led to a respectable online presence to disseminate information about the department and complement its web page.

MOBILE AGENCY APPS (EXTERNAL COMMUNITY-FACING)

All the cool kids on the block have their own mobile apps. In all seriousness, there are some advantages to investing in an external-facing agency app. A quick internet search will turn up several companies. Choose a company that has developed public safety apps. I went with Kevin Cummings, vice president of sales with theSheriffApp.com, based on the company's experience in the law enforcement and municipal/county government space.

You want your app to work for you. Good starting points for functions and content include contact information, tip submission, and a leader's message. Embed your social media feeds and carve out a space for public reports. Services provided, recruiting corners, and community engagement can round out the buttons. Blogs can also be included. Allowing your community to search crime records and sex offenders adds to transparency.

REPORTS

Reports bolster both credibility and transparency. Think about a nonfiction author writing a book. It establishes them as an authority on their topic. In the same vein, we are the authority in public safety. A well-written report can be used as a marketing and branding tool and serve as a business card where we "market" our core services and programs. Community members learn about what we do. A report shows residents what we have to offer. It documents the level of crime. It accounts for the resources elected officials and the governing body provide. With complete editorial control over the makeup, content, and visual display of facts, figures, and photos, many opportunities exist to highlight your agency in reports.

Reports come in all shapes and sizes and fulfill many purposes. Some reports may be legislatively mandated, while your boss may assign others. Should you publish a printed version, an electronic one, or both? This section challenges leaders and strategic communication advisors to innovate and think outside the box to create reports that have meaning and value for the consumer.

ANNUAL REPORTS

Annual reports showcase the great things that our people do. Commit to doing them. They demonstrate what your agency did with the tax dollars entrusted to it and serve as a historical record of what happened during the year. Releasing an annual report before the next budget process is a great way to rally support for your budget asks. For yearly report templates, go to www.policepio.com.

MONTHLY, QUARTERLY, AND OTHER REPORTS

Monthly and reports issued at other frequencies may consist of productivity, crime, or other metrics. Many agencies already produce detailed monthly reports that are kept internally. Look for ways to strategically share appropriate information with the community. Examples include a monthly report card containing a different photo each month and quantitative data on property crimes, violent crimes, traffic stops, arrests, crashes, calls for service, social media reach, and community events. Another example may be a monthly newsletter with a professional magazine appearance containing stories, events, and performance measures. Let your imagination flow and check out other agencies that are doing these products well.

USE OF FORCE

This falls within the transparency bucket. While most large agencies produce a quarterly or annual report that evaluates force, leaders need to determine the purpose and what data will be included. Data without stories or context will not be received well. This is an opportunity for agencies to talk about training, tools, and de-escalation efforts. Highlight narratives that show the level of compliance as matched with the level of reasonable force. A use-of-force report presented in a format that residents can easily understand may lead to greater support and cooperation from the community.

PURSUIT STATISTICAL SUMMARIES

Another area that bolsters transparency deals with how the organization manages vehicular pursuits. Regardless of your policy, there are ways to showcase how officers deal with suspects who evade. Include stories and perspectives with the data points. Talk about the policy at your department. Discuss training initiatives related to emergency vehicle operation.

ANNUAL COMPLAINT SUMMARIES

While commonplace in large urban agencies, leaders need to determine if there is value in providing data on the number of complaints, types of complaints, and their disposition. My recommendation is to use aggregate data versus naming individualized employees. This is because these types of summaries can provide informative feedback on possible trends occurring in the organization when analyzing aggregate data. Find out what works in your community. For example, if you never receive requests for this information, you may decide this would be irrelevant to your community.

ANNUAL COMMENDATION SUMMARIES

Prepare annual commendation summaries if you plan on releasing annual complaint summaries. Why not one over the other? As a profession, we need to appear authentic in our communications. If we only report the good, we will develop credibility issues, and citizens may believe we are only on a public relations crusade. If we only report the bad, we are missing opportunities to provide balance and perspective—the fact that sustained misconduct does not reflect the whole agency, and the vast majority of police officers do an exceptional job.

WEB CONTENT

Websites take work to maintain a fresh appearance. A static website that never changes will ensure that visitors don't return. Make sure you keep contact information relevant and up to date. A website is ideally suited for the placement of your public reports. As a resource library, citizens can be directed to review information at a central location on a webpage.

Place your news into two funnels. One page should house your formal news releases and media advisories. Another page should have proactive stories that citizens can click into, preferably the front landing page. Additionally, embed a trailer video or the latest video content onto the main page. Social media icons can also be prominently displayed to drive traffic to your networking sites.

While many cities and counties require departments to follow specific branding protocols, check if custom headers with changing short videos and banner photos are allowed.

BLUEPRINT—CHAPTER 11

FIFTEEN THINGS NEEDED ON EVERY WEBSITE

1. Dynamic scrolling banners with short videos and cool photos

2. Story boxes with photos, sound bites, and BLUF messaging

3. The latest news stories, written with storytelling principles

4. Official news releases and media advisories

5. Embedded YouTube channel, trailer, or select video

6. An "About Section" featuring the leader's message and specific content showcasing the executive's commitment to communication and engagement

7. Contact information for command staff, commanders, and shift supervisors

8. Recruiting section with hiring process, opportunities, salary, benefits, and what sets the agency apart from others

9. Community programs section

10. Public reports section

11. Volunteer section

12. Divisions and services offered to the community

13. A section for submitting tips

14. Open records/FOIA request portal

15. Commend and complain section

BLUEPRINT: WEEKLY, MONTHLY, QUARTERLY, BIANNUAL, AND ANNUAL REPORTS

While each agency should determine which reports to release publicly, these are a few examples of reports that can be sanitized for public consumption:

- Weekly beat reports
- Monthly or bimonthly crime reports
- Monthly performance reports (removing individual officer data and reporting aggregate traffic stops, arrests, community contacts, etc.)
- Quarterly use of force reports
- Biannual license plate reader reports
- Annual pursuit summary report
- Annual department report
- Annual performance management report (discipline and commendations)
- Annual racial data collection report

PART III

WHAT COMES NEXT?

CHAPTER 12

THE ART OF STRATEGIC COMMUNICATION

I n sunny San Diego in the fall of 2012, thousands of individuals gathered for the annual IACP Conference. As a newbie in the communications world, I was in awe as I walked through the convention center. The sheer number of people was nothing to shake a stick at. And by the way, I had thought this conference was only for police chiefs, right? A few seasoned PIOs I had met previously in Vancouver invited me to attend the Public Information Officers Section—a dedicated space under the greater IACP umbrella with training and networking focused on messaging.

I learned so much and forged strong relationships with people doing things right that I have never missed a conference since that day. During the many annual conferences in places such as Philadelphia, Orlando, Chicago, San Diego, and Dallas, one constant has always remained—the relentless pursuit of excellence through strategic communication and messaging.

This is where I networked with innovators who set the tone and culture for what today's modern law enforcement agency ascends to. Julie Parker, who was working at the Prince George's County Police Department at the time and is now president and CEO of Julie Parker Communications, brought a unique skill set as a former reporter to the field of policing. From sharing how to interact with media to navigating crises, her candid advice has reinforced the need to approach communications from a strategic vantage point.

Julia Hill, former Communications Director for the City of Virginia Beach and author of many contemporary publications, has imparted expertise across various public safety organizations. Most notably, through her writing and teaching, Julia reminds our leaders of the importance of strategic communication when dealing with news media and the public.

The list could continue. The point is that many trailblazers have carved a path of success when thinking and communicating strategically. Strategic thinking involves receiving information, making assessments, developing a plan, executing the strategy, and evaluating its effectiveness. Remember ACE—assess, choose a plan, execute, and evaluate. When we engage in strategic thinking, the natural evolution is strategic communication—the tools, principles, strategies, channels, and guiding plan to accomplish one's goals and objectives.

This final chapter will review some of the earlier key concepts while also introducing what is on the horizon for communicators and leaders.

COFFEE BREAK

I remember having coffee with a group of police chiefs who had given decades to our profession. The topic of news media came up, and the chiefs reminisced about days gone by when they rarely had to deal with a reporter. They also unequivocally denounced the adoption of social media, which had not existed during the early years of their careers. The conversation reaffirmed that every aspect of telling the story of policing has changed—for better or worse, you can be the judge.

Telling our story is now more important than ever. Dealing

with a global pandemic, messaging throughout natural disasters, historic floods and fires, monster hurricanes, school shootings, and other high-profile critical incidents that are emotionally charged—the role of communicators has evolved to the point of a necessity. There is no going back to the perceived past, as referred to by some of the gray-haired chiefs that morning. The role of leaders and communicators within the policing profession has continued to expand. At the same time, law enforcement has also experienced some potential barriers to achieving success regarding public information.

The state of news affairs has dramatically shifted over the past decade with the proliferation of social media. Communities are more connected than ever through the plethora of online news blogs, social media posts, and the twenty-four-hour news cycle that constantly broadcasts information to the public. This is not to say that the thirst for immediate awareness of what's happening around us is entirely negative. However, police executives must harness the power of traditional and social media platforms to tell the profession's story and stay in front of news-related incidents that can descend upon an organization.

Every law enforcement organization must have a well-planned, strategic crisis communication plan and an established, written media relations policy. This will allow employees to understand the significance of good public relations concerning law enforcement events and activities. A robust strategic communication plan also assists with promoting positive community relations, generates greater public support for budgetary requests and initiatives, and builds legitimacy with news organizations. This plan should have defined priorities and goals. Rapid response strategies for the upper echelon of leadership and advisors should be incorporated for consistent application and timely release to the public and media.

Communicating internally can significantly affect the agency's drive to improve. A trained communicator and well-versed agency head can play a critical role in ensuring organizational team members have access to what is happening. A connected strategic communication advisor can also assist with policymaking by improving internal and external communication standards that seek input and buy-in from employees and community stakeholders. Here are some important items to consider and embrace to fully realize the power and influence of strategic communication.

BIGGEST MISTAKE IN MESSAGING

The biggest mistake is approaching a topic, incident, or crisis without a clear strategy to message your community through the media. Leaders and strategic communication advisors must:

- Have a clear goal
- Identify and understand their target audience
- Articulate a sound bite and key messages
- Share information on the appropriate channel

Not having a clear strategy results in wasted energy and nonalignment of messages with your strategic communication and crisis plans and can set the organization up for a major communication failure. Don't squander an opportunity to define your core messages.

RIGHT PLACE AT THE RIGHT TIME

Part of embracing the art of strategic communication is being at the right place at the right time. There are two takeaways for executives and communicators. First, as leaders, we must leave our office and hit the streets. We must be aware of what is happening and not lose touch with the troops. The community needs to see us on calls, not just events. For strategic communication advisors, you need to encourage the boss to wear the uniform, jump in a vehicle, and answer some calls for service. You are enhancing the perception of leading from the front and putting the leader in a position to communicate strategically on incidents, police work, and community connections.

The second part involves ensuring employees can document incidents and events. A picture is worth way more than just words alone. A video is even better. To share the event with the community, having someone at the Friday night football game to capture a first responder appreciation game is money in the bank. Train your staff to capture photos and videos. Remind them to tell you the great things that are going on. Encourage self-reporting of great arrests and duties. As ambassadors for the agency, your employees are a force multiplier in the art of strategic communication.

A good mentor gave me a poster when I was appointed police chief. It depicts General George S. Patton with his phrase, "No good decision was ever made in a swivel chair." I am often reminded of the meaning when I enter the office each day. I regularly wear the uniform to respond, if needed, to back up one of my teammates. I am also reminded of the need for leaders to get out of the office by trendsetters like Steve Dye, former police chief in Grand Prairie, Texas. I can remember turning on the news a couple of times and seeing Steve putting the handcuffs on a suspect with his officers. Strategically, these stories resonate with the community and police officers.

OPPOSITE OF STRATEGIC COMMUNICATION

While we continue defining what strategic communication ought to be, it is sometimes easier to point out what it is not. You have heard the adage, "flying by the seat of your pants." This plagues many agencies, communicators, and leaders. These individuals are going through the motions—cranking out news releases, doing a few interviews, sharing some posts, and producing a video once a month. But they are not thinking or executing strategically. They are not intentional about the content and timing of said activities. By not adhering to a strategic communication plan, there's a lot of wasted effort, minimal reach, and a dismal amount of video views.

Another pitfall is focusing on just the numbers. Everyone likes to tout follower counts, likes, and impressions. But what the heck does a hundred thousand "impressions" mean anyway? Does the number of YouTube subscribers mean you are reaching your intended audience? While law enforcement, and government for that matter, love statistics and numbers, I would argue that we need to look at definitive outcomes.

Instead of solely reporting followers, can we look at how many people became better educated on what to do during traffic stops? Based on our social media recruiting strategy of releasing a video, can we assess our increase in applications received? Were we able to move the needle to increase the public's trust in the policing institution based on a social media campaign? Could a decrease in impaired driving be tied back to an extensive video campaign on education and deterrence?

This sounds good, but how do we measure definitive outcomes?

STREET CREDIBILITY

I developed a system that has been used in multiple agencies. Sorry, another acronym, but this is what keeps me on track. It's all about seeking street credibility with your communications.

Statistics

Traffic

Reach

Effectiveness

Education

Trust

The first measure deals with statistics. It's a simple formula. For each post, video, or content, take the total number of interactions (likes, favorites, comments, and views), and divide by the total number of followers or subscribers on the networking site. This will give you a baseline for comparing against future content. Based on this number, you can create goals on how much you desire to increase the percentage of interaction.

The second measure deals with traffic. This could be website traffic, such as page views and clicks, mobile app downloads, or click-through rates from posts to other content pages.

The next measure is reach. Most social media networks provide organic versus paid reach (I assume most agencies do not pay to promote their content unless it's recruiting stuff). I find that impressions and reach are not meaningful for most of the analytics that I do, however, some agencies want to showcase these types of numerical values. Many agencies use reach, impressions, and views as a measure to gauge "brand awareness."

The next measure is effectiveness. You can measure effectiveness by looking at crime rates before and after a campaign is completed. For example, if you instituted a task force operation focusing on crime at local motels, measure the crime before the communication starts and then remeasure after a few weeks to see if your content strategy is working (or it could be your enforcement strategy, too).

Education is the next measure. This could be a numerical value, such as adding participants to the next Citizens Police Academy. Or, it could be an anecdotal measure, such as written correspondence showcasing how the campaign increased education on a particular topic.

Trust is the final and most important measure. This is where you can put on your academic hat. Using traditional research methods, agencies survey community members before and after a campaign. The goal is to increase trust in the agency. Surveys can contain several questions to measure whether trust was elevated. A leader can quickly ascertain whether the content or program increased trust—the whole point of engaging in communications in the first place.

Ultimately, you will have developed some street cred related to strategic communication. With that cred comes bragging rights that your team is intentionally benchmarking and measuring outcomes on the content they develop and distribute. The measures provide more value than static numbers. They can also be incorporated into budgetary planning processes to demonstrate the need to procure communications equipment or add a dedicated advisor to manage communications.

VOIR DIRE

Speak the truth. Always tell the truth. As leaders, we only have our credibility; once it's gone, our careers are over. From a communications perspective, it means that we stick to the facts. When the community or media demand an answer on a topic we cannot disclose, we acknowledge that we cannot discuss the topic in question—versus saying, "No comment."

WHERE THERE'S SMOKE, THERE'S FIRE

Everyone knows this metaphor. From a strategic mindset, this can assist an agency in identifying and responding to potential issues. Leaders and strategic communication advisors need multiple ways to monitor the brand.

First, social media monitoring is a must. And not just from a preservation of records standpoint. I am talking about establishing keywords, phrases, and brand elements to alert your team that someone is talking about your agency, brand, image, and reputation. Alerts can serve to determine what happened, or at least what someone is reporting happened, and allow your agency to review facts and decide whether to respond and, if so, how to respond. Imagine the power of the organization when you are aware of what is happening across social media. One of the biggest impediments to using social media cited by executives is dealing with all the noise, brand attacks, and misinformation that abounds. Embracing social media monitoring helps agencies manage these types of challenges.

Second, having a team of employee advocates bodes for your future success from a knowledge standpoint. Employees are out in the community, hear things, and can alert the agency of potential troubles. I would much rather have an employee tell me that a use of force incident was recorded by a dozen hostile people versus not having any awareness. Training your people to be observers and monitors will undoubtedly assist the team in becoming aware of misinformation or challenging topics. It could also take the form of an employee who sees something distributed by local media that is incorrect. The agency could contact the station and correct the story by providing the correct information to the right people.

Third, traditional media monitoring should be a priority for any agency that responds to more than one thousand calls a year—which probably encompasses most agencies in America. Why? How can you be sure that your sound bite and information are being correctly disseminated to the public? Some news outlets post a web version of the video and story. But in some cases, they don't. As leaders and advisors, we must monitor local, state, regional, national, and international media. I don't care what company you use; get something in place. The money spent can provide peace of mind that your strategic messaging is hitting the right audiences.

Alerts will provide you with awareness and time. By identifying potential problems and having time on your side, your team can make a more informed decision on approaching the issue and putting the fire out. I cannot tell you how often I have wished for more awareness and time on an issue in my career. In many cases, my awareness came from a media inquiry about a Facebook post or video on YouTube, which afforded me little to no time to strategize and deal with the issue. Starting behind the curve presents its own set of challenges. Knowledge and awareness are at the core of strategic communication.

JUDGE, JURY, AND EXECUTIONER

On the one hand, the leader represents the judge, jury, and executioner as it relates to communications strategy—meaning that you are ultimately in charge of what is released and how it's released, regardless of whether you delegate this responsibility to another individual. On the other hand, you are neither the judge, jury, nor executioner regarding how people interpret and receive your communications. The community will be the judge as to the value and meaningfulness of your communication efforts. The community will also be the jury on what works and what doesn't. This includes determining whether your communication style and delivery were appropriate and legitimate in their eyes. Lastly, the community will execute whether they rally behind the agency or issue accountability demands. This is critical during controversies.

DON'T CARE ABOUT SOCIAL MEDIA?

I shrug my shoulders when executives and advisors say they don't care about social media. Guess what? No one cares that you don't care about social media. It's not about you. This is where I would tell my kids, "Suck it up, buttercup." As leaders and advisors, we need to set the appropriate tone that embraces the twenty-first century—the world of social media. It's not going away. Yes, social networking sites may change, and Elon Musk got rid of the bird, but the idea of connecting and interacting through digital platforms where people create, share, and exchange information and thoughts in the virtual world is here to stay.

Law enforcement must embrace the positive side of social media, navigate the challenging side of social media, and manage the negative side. Just because you may be a Baby Boomer or Generation Xer who has never used social media doesn't mean you should avoid connecting with audiences in the digital world of other Baby Boomers, Gen Xers, millennials, and members of Gen Z and Gen Alpha. That's like saying, "In the good ole days, we carried a notepad and radio to answer calls." Great—I, too, came into policing before computers were widespread. Still, part of being great at the art of strategic communication means that we adapt to technology and tools to get our messages out.

ME, MYSELF, AND I

One of my goals in writing this book was to present ideas and strategies that can be utilized by law enforcement leaders, strategic communication advisors, and public information officers. I know that many readers are one-person shows. And I further understand that many of you have other competing and important tasks. In addition to large organizations with a team of communication professionals, graphic artists, videographers, and social media experts, our profession needed a resource guide that could be implemented in the smallest departments. That's where the *Art of Strategic Communication* comes in.

This guidebook will undoubtedly assist in your agency's most challenging cases. My task for you is to approach your communications strategically. This will put you in front of emerging incidents. Strategic communications are surefire ways to build community trust and internal legitimacy with employees. A plan to deal with unexpected situations will lead to a greater likelihood of positive outcomes for the agency.

Can you do this as a police chief, sheriff, commissioner, or leader? Yes. Tell yourself now that you have the tools and insights to be successful. There will be challenges and failures along the way. That's part of life. Leveraging communication tools and approaching situations with a strategic mindset will improve the survivability of your tenure, build employee trust, and lead to better service in your community—especially during controversial incidents.

Commit to networking and learning. Attend conferences and training related to communications. As a leader and advisor, join national groups with like-minded individuals striving to get this right. Don't be afraid to try new things. Develop a strategic communication plan. Write a crisis communication plan. Work on a branding strategy, if needed. Share your successes and failures with others in the profession so that we can collectively become better. Case studies are incredible ways to learn. Like an after-action report, hearing how someone approached a crisis can assist peers in developing best practices.

MEDIA—FRIEND OR FOE?

Media are neither friend nor foe (yes, they can be friendly or mean, but that's not what I am talking about). It is their job to be objective, providing the facts and then allowing the public to interpret them and make up their own minds. Major incidents and crises covered by the media have four phases:

- Phase 1—Reporting—In the initial reports on a major incident or crisis, the media will report official information from your agency, witness accounts, and perceived impacts on the community.
- Phase 2—Ally—Initial and subsequent reporting is typically favorable as the incident or crisis evolves. This occurs through highlighting what your agency did to keep the community safe.
- Phase 3—Adversary—With more attention to the incident or crisis, "experts" critique the response and explain what your agency should have known or done to resolve the situation. This phase is where the open records requests flow in from media.
- Phase 4—Aftermath—Once the initial phases have run their course, the incident or crisis enters the aftermath stage. This is where the news shifts to other current incidents or events, and your agency moves out of the news cycle. It is possible that news pegs, such as court appearances, funerals, and other items of currency related to the incident or crisis, will generate some additional coverage.

Leaders and strategic communication advisors should recognize and anticipate these phases of news coverage. Objectivity is still the standard for journalism, regardless of which phase. Have I developed lifelong friendships with some of the reporters and news personnel with whom my career has regularly crossed paths? Absolutely. It's about respecting the ethical line of professionalism when interacting with media in a business setting.

FUTURE OF COMMUNICATION

As communication tools advance, agencies will still need to message communities. I was in a meeting in 2023 with several employees representing the fire department and animal services team. As we discussed social media engagement, a millennial who oversaw social media for their teams said to the group, "I am having ChatGPT create my content for Facebook." Those of us in the room with a few gray hairs looked at each other in surprise. The employee started explaining that she writes some basic facts into the AI program, and it generates content that can be posted.

ChatGPT is a generative artificial intelligence (AI) that can respond to user prompts.[62] AI is starting to emerge in serious nationwide debates. Where will this lead? It's likely going to alter the way we interact with writing. There will be organizations that explore the functionality of AI as a conversational tool. Already, society is seeing social media companies publish articles on how AI can "streamline your workflows, automate tasks, and never worry about finding the perfect caption again."[63] Companies are even popping up to provide AI-generated captions and content ideas for social media networks.

I think leaders and advisors must approach this topic carefully without knowing where computer programming or AI is getting the information to populate user content. Our agencies are built on trust and facts. AI has pulled information from

erroneous sources in well-documented cases, publishing inac-
curate data. I, for one, will default to the traditional method of
manually creating content for the time being. I would advise
fact-checking any AI-generated posts and revising posts to
fit your messaging strategy to maintain credibility since your
agency name will still be associated with the posts.

HOMEWORK—COMMIT TO CREATING STRATEGIC COMMUNICATION AND CRISIS PLANS

I know that it's been said many times throughout this book,
but I challenge our leaders and advisors to develop the necessary and important plans to enhance your strategic communication activities: a strategic communications plan and a crisis communication plan. Templates are available. A strategic
communication plan orients your agency's goals and objectives under a unified document to support your strategy in
approaching communication—written, digital, video, spoken,
and other facets. A crisis communication plan is invaluable
when crises arise, and emotions run high. The crisis communication plan is a roadmap of things to consider, things to
do, when to do them, and how to do them. And last, develop
a written media relations policy. This is your homework to
embrace the art of strategic communication fully. (You can
find these templates at policepio.com for free).

DUSTY BOOKSHELF

There is always change in law enforcement. Leaders come and
go. Strategic communication advisors move around. Agencies
routinely make changes to their communication efforts. One
of the reasons for writing this book is to assist leaders and

communicators who answer the call. Whether this is your first appointment as an executive or you landed the job as a former news reporter, don't let this book get lost on a dusty bookshelf. Keep it handy. It's meant to be a resource guide that can be quickly accessed. Committing oneself to the art of strategic communication includes improving your focus through learning. A recent poll cited that 26 percent of adults reading a book in the past year said they enjoyed learning, gaining knowledge, and discovering information most.[64]

STRATEGIC COMMUNICATORS MAKE GREAT LEADERS

If you have been in the business for a while, you have probably heard the saying that PIOs make great chiefs. I believe that premise. I have experienced many successes directly tied to my prior media and public relations role. Communicating effectively, with a strategic focus, assists law enforcement agencies. Have no fear if you are the top cop without a prior formal communications role or training. Now that you have found strategic resources, you will be a better leader! Communities are better served by leaders who can communicate—strategically. And departments are better served.

If your goal is to continue climbing the ladder with aspirations to lead a law enforcement agency or improve the brand of your current agency, the tools, tips, and blueprints in this book will help you get there.

THE END GOAL

The goal is to create an environment where your employees and community are participatory and empowered to help create safer neighborhoods with the public safety team. The roadmap to elicit cooperation and create an army of public safety advocates is rooted in strategic communication objectives. From internal communication to outwardly facing strategies, agencies must work to bridge the gap, create partnerships across diverse audiences, and engage in constructive dialogue with employees and communities. The end goal of reaffirming confidence in the agency's value and purpose, enhancing trust that lasts for generations, and projecting dignity and respect throughout all law enforcement interactions is foundationally supported by mastering the *Art of Strategic Communication.*

APPENDICES

FURTHER WAYS TO MASTER THE ART OF STRATEGIC COMMUNICATION

INTERESTED IN LEARNING MORE ABOUT THE ART OF STRATEGIC COMMUNICATION?

Christopher Cook and Zhivonni Cook, owners of First Responder Media Consultants, LLC, offer training workshops and keynote presentations. Services include executive coaching, media relations training, thought leader consulting, and crisis management. Main areas of expertise include social media, police-media relations, managing critical incidents, navigating serious officer misconduct, controversial deadly force encounters, mass shooting and active shooter incidents, crisis mitigation, annual report publication, graphic design, brochure design, monthly report design and publication, professional photography services, video production, critical incident video preparation, recruiting strategies, community engagement, relational policing initiatives, podcasting content development, seminar-style teaching, virtual learning academies, strategic planning, crisis communication plans, development of interview skill sets, public speaking enhancement, and many other law enforcement-centric topics for leaders and strategic communication advisors.

To learn more about our services or request training, email chief@policepio.com, text at 817-657-7296 or visit our website:

www.policepio.com
LinkedIn: www.linkedin.com/in/ChiefCook/
X (Twitter): @CookTX and @StrategyPIO

PUT *THE ART OF STRATEGIC COMMUNICATION* IN THE HANDS OF YOUR TEAM, CLASS, OR ORGANIZATION.

Agencies, training academies, and universities can obtain bulk order pricing of this book through the publisher at info@indiebooksintl.com or www.indiebooksintl.com or the author at chief@policepio.com.

ABOUT CO-INSTRUCTOR ZHIVONNI COOK, POLICE OFFICER

Zhivonni Cook is a subject matter expert in the field of social media for law enforcement and media relations for public safety. As a law enforcement veteran with twenty-four years of service in the profession, she has numerous skills in the field of public information. Zhivonni began her career in law enforcement in 2000 and served as a police officer for the Arlington (Texas) Police Department. She oversaw the agency's social media platforms and citizen engagement efforts, leading to three consecutive years of awards by the Texas Center for Digital Government for the most innovative use of social media.

Since 2019, she has served as a sworn strategic communication advisor for the Mansfield (Texas) Police Department. Before her policing career, she worked in public relations for the Six Flags Entertainment Corporation. Zhivonni has a bachelor of arts degree in communication from Trenton State College (now The College of New Jersey).

ACKNOWLEDGEMENTS

This book has been a work in progress for several years. Speaking at conferences across the country on the importance of police-media relations, proactive storytelling, and community engagement, many police leaders continually asked me for a reference book on the "how" and the "why." When we can answer the "why," our organizations are better at providing public safety through the "how." Putting pen to paper requires intense focus, dedication, and time.

First and foremost, credit goes to my beautiful wife, Zhivonni Cook. As a police officer and expert communications advisor, she was instrumental in helping me structure the content and layout. She is my better half, with a creative mind and uncanny ability to co-teach this stuff in a way that captivates audiences.

I also want to thank my family, who continued to push me to the finish line. Writing takes time, which is a precious commodity. My mom, LaNette Cook; mother-in-law, Vasha Kurokawa; father-in-law, Wayne Kurokawa; son, Benjamin; and stepdaughters, Torre and Isabella, always supported and challenged me to complete this project.

My publisher, CEO Henry DeVries of Indie Books International Inc., was patient and encouraged me along the journey to get to a publishable manuscript. I owe Henry a great deal of gratitude for his insights and structure. Devin DeVries, vice president of production and promotion, along with Suzanne Hagen, director of promotions, ensured that I had everything that was needed every step of the way including the cover design, interior layout, and book elements. Lisa

Lucas, managing editor, was instrumental in preparing the manuscript for formal publication. The entire team of Indie Books International took extreme interest in producing the highest quality book that would resonate with lifelong learners of our noble profession.

To the consummate law enforcement professionals around the country who put their lives on the line every single day, I salute each one of you and the honorable service you provide. This book was written to showcase your outstanding work and build strong bonds between our police officers and the public we serve.

To my peer police chiefs, sheriffs, and law enforcement leaders, who always strive to get public information right from the start and ask for help when needed, thank you. Your exemplary work is acknowledged in this book.

To the public information officers and strategic communication advisors who perform a vital and necessary service to our society, I have learned amazing things from you that were most certainly incorporated into this book. Many of you have directly impacted my success over the years. It would be futile to try and list every person who invested in my success or provided guidance. The following groups and organizations collaborated, shared, and imparted wisdom to me that allowed me to give back to our profession: the National Information Officers Association, the International Association of Chiefs of Police—Public Information Officers Section, the Major Cities Chiefs Association—Public Information Officers Committee, the Police Executive Research Forum, the Texas Police Chiefs Association, the FBI National Command Course Association, the Institute for Law Enforcement Administration Alumni Association, the Caruth Policing Institute, the Bill Blackwood Law Enforcement Management Institute of Texas, and the North Texas Public Information Officers Group. Thank you!

ABOUT THE AUTHOR

Christopher Cook is best known for his contributions to the field of public safety communications and police-media relations. Rising through the ranks from Deputy Sheriff in Tarrant County, Texas, Deputy Police Chief in Arlington, Texas, to Chief of Police in White Settlement, Texas, he draws from real-world experience over the past three decades to serve as an expert instructor, executive coach, and mentor. Over ten thousand leaders and students have received his instruction at various classes and conferences since 2011.

Specializing in strategic communication, crisis management, and media relations, Chief Cook has published and collaborated on more than three dozen professional journal articles, magazine articles, and law enforcement publications. Executive teaching engagements have spanned the country, including adjunct professor assignments at colleges and universities.

Chief Cook was one of only a handful of law enforcement leaders from across the country who received an invitation from and testified before the President's Commission on Law Enforcement and the Administration of Justice's Community Trust and Respect for Law Enforcement Panel in 2020. A consummate leader, he currently teaches at Sam Houston State University's Bill Blackwood Law Enforcement Management Institute of Texas. As part of this multiyear appointment, every police chief in Texas—representing 2,762 agencies—attends his four-hour strategic communication course.

Chief Cook serves on the Caruth Police Institute Executive Advisory Board, the Institute for Law Enforcement Administration Advisory Board, the Executive Board of the Federal Bureau of Investigation National Command Course Association, and the Fort Worth Airpower Council. He is the past president of the National Information Officers Association, past chair of the International Association of Chiefs of Police—PIO Section, and past chair of the Major Cities Chiefs Association—PIO Committee.

Educational attainment includes a master of arts degree in criminology and criminal justice from the University of Texas at Arlington and completion of PhD core-level coursework at Tarleton State University, a Texas A&M University System member. He is a graduate of the FBI National Command Course Session #4, the Police Executive Research Forum's Senior Management Institute for Police Session #63, Bill Blackwood Law Enforcement Management Institute of Texas Leadership Command College Session #67, and 96th School of Police Supervision at the Institute for Law Enforcement Administration. He is also a member of Leadership North Texas Class #15 and the 2024 Certified Public Manager Program at Texas State University.

As of publication, he is the only police chief in the world to receive the prestigious Leadership in Public Information Management Award from the IACP. He also received the ConnectedCOPS Social Media Leadership Award and the Most Innovative Use of Social Media award in Texas for three consecutive years.

Raised in the Dallas-Fort Worth metropolitan area, he is an avid photographer, reader, and frequent traveler to the Hawaiian Islands. He also enjoys spending time with family and friends. As a USAF veteran, he advocates for our men and women in the armed forces by volunteering at the Naval Air Station Joint Reserve Base Fort Worth.

APPENDIX D

WORKS CITED AND ENDNOTES

1   Michael Nila and Stephen R. Covey, et al., *The Nobility of Policing* (Salt Lake City: Franklin Quest, 2008).

2   "Current Statistics," Texas Commission on Law Enforcement, https://www.tcole.texas.gov/content/current-statistics, accessed October 25, 2023.

3   Jim Collins, *Good to Great: Why Some Companies Make the Leap and Others Don't* (New York, HarperBusiness, 2001).

4   Simon Sinek, *Start with Why: How Great Leaders Inspire Everyone to Take Action* (London: Penguin Books, 2011).

5   Katie Nelson, "Masters of All—How the Skills of Modern-Day PIOs Are Revolutionizing Information Sharing," *Police Chief* Magazine, accessed November 12, 2023, https://www.police1.com/media-relations/articles/managing-the-media-when-crisis-hits-your-hometown-WKFGLJsESliDU856/

6   Theron Bowman, https://www.cailaw.org/media/files/ILEA/Bios/theron-bowman.pdf

7   Judy Pal, "Managing the Media When Crisis Hits Your Hometown," Police1, May 21, 2021, https://www.police1.com/media-relations/articles/managing-the-media-when-crisis-hits-your-hometown-WKFGLJsESliDU856/.

8   Phil Helsel, "Interim Emergency Management Hired After Deadly Maui Fires," *NBC News*, August 25, 2023, https://www.nbcnews.com/news/weather/interim-emergency-management-director-hired-deadly-wildfires-rcna101933

9   "Digital Edition: What cops want in 2022", Police1, February 28, 2022, https://www.police1.com/police-products/body-cameras/articles/digital-edition-what-cops-want-in-2022-CkFK0jUZrpFOUjeR/

10   Zig Ziglar, "If You Want to Reach a Goal," The Ziglar Experience, accessed October 26, 2023, https://www.ziglar.com/quotes/if-you-want-reach-goal/.

11   Collins, *Good to Great*.

12   Chuck Wexler, et al., *Good to Great Policing: Application of Business Management Principles in the Public Sector* (Washington, DC: Police Executive Research Forum, 2007).

13   David Mikkelson, "Dragnet: 'Just the Facts. Ma'am,'" Snopes, March 29, 2002, https://www.snopes.com/fact-check/just-the-facts/.

14   Julie Parker(@JulieParkerComm), "If you publicly describe your organization as transparent, whether you work in communications or not, ask yourself if that's a true statement. If it isn't, encourage leadership to eliminate that description from your messaging," Twitter, January 22, 2022, 3:06 a.m.

15   "Reporter Salary in United States," Indeed, accessed October 30, 2023, https://www.indeed.com/career/reporter/salaries.

16   Lisa Marchand, "What Is Readability and Why Should Content Editors Care About It?" Center for Plain Language, March 22, 2017, https://centerforplainlanguage.org/what-is-readability/.

17   Center for Plain Language, "What is readability and why should content editors care about it?" March 22, 2017, https://centerforplainlanguage.org/what-is-readability/

18   "2022–2023 Nielsen DMA Ranking," US TVDB, accessed November 12, 2023, https://ustvdb.com/seasons/2022-23/markets/.

19   Gail Pennyback and Kenneth White, "Focus on Social Media," LEB, February 21, 2021, https://leb.fbi.gov/articles/focus/focus-on-social-media-effectively-managing-messages

20   Tom Stafford, "Why Bad News Dominates the Headlines," *BBC*, July 28, 2014, https://www.bbc.com/future/article/20140728-why-is-all-the-news-bad.

21   "The Eight Top Social Media Sites You Should Prioritize in 2023," Adobe Express, August 10, 2022, https://www.adobe.com/express/learn/blog/top-social-media-sites.

22 Alexandra Barinka, "Meta's Instagram Users Reach 2 Billion, Closing In On Facebook." *Bloomberg News*, October 26, 2022, https://www.bloomberg.com/news/articles/2022-10-26/meta-s-instagram-users-reach-2-billion-closing-in-on-facebook?embedded-checkout=true

23 Brent Barnhart, "Social Media Demographics to Inform Your Brand's Strategy in 2023," Sprout Social, April 28, 2023, https://sproutsocial.com/insights/new-social-media-demographics/.

24 Adobe Express, "The Eight Top."

25 Adobe Express, "The Eight Top."

26 Christina Newberry, "2023 Facebook Algorithm: How to get your content seen," Hootsuite (blog), February 22, 2023, https://blog.hootsuite.com/facebook-algorithm/.

27 "Content Is Fire. Social Media Is Gasoline," Strategic America, March 11, 2014, https://www.strategicamerica.com/blog/2014/03/content-fire-social-media-gasoline/..

28 Shane Barker (@shane_barker), "The goal of social media is to turn customers into your personal evangelist," November 12, 2015, 6:52 p.m., https://twitter.com/shane_barker/status/664999126405242880.

29 Seth Godin, https://financialbrandforum.com/seth-godin/, accessed November 4, 2023.

30 Chris Hsiung (@Sheriff_Hsiung), "See a few examples of the PIO fame effect over the years. Doesn't reflect well on the PIO or the agency," March 20, 2019, E

31 "Inspiring social media quotes for beginners," InfluencerMarketing.Ai, accessed November 12, 2023, https://influencermarketing.ai/inspiring-social-media-quotes-for-beginners/.

32 William P. Barr, "Attorney General William P. Barr's Remarks on Mr. George Floyd and Civil Unrest," Office of Public Affairs, US Department of Justice, June 4, 2020, https://www.justice.gov/opa/speech/attorney-general-william-p-barr-s-remarks-mr-george-floyd-and-civil-unrest.

33 Cornelius v. NAACP Leg. Def. & Ed. Fund, Inc., 473 U.S. 788, 802 (1985); Attwood v. Clemons, 526 F. Supp. 3d 1152, 1170 (N.D. Fla. 2021).

34   People for the Ethical Treatment of Animals v. Tabak, No. 21-CV-2380 (BAH), 2023 WL 2809867, at 14 (D.D.C. Mar. 31, 2023). Caroline Bush, "Legal Q&A." *Texas Town & City,* vol. 109, no. 10, 1 Dec. 2023, p. 22-28.

35   Jeff Thompson, *warr;or21* (Research Triangle Park, NC: lulu.com, 2020).

36   Scott Gordon, "A Conversation With Four North Texas Police Officers," KXAS-TV NBC5, June 12, 2020.

37   J. N. Kapferer, *The New Strategic Brand Management: Creating and Sustaining Brand Equity Long Term,* 4th ed. (New York: Kogan Page Publishers, 2008).

38   Tom R. Tyler, *Why People Obey the Law,* rev. ed. (Princeton, NJ: Princeton University Press, 2006).

39   Lorraine Mazerolle, Sarah Bennett, Jacqueline Davis, Elise Sargeant, and Matthew Manning, "Legitimacy in Policing: A Systematic Review," Campbell Systematic Reviews 9 (2012): 1.

40   Los Angeles Police Department, LAPD Motto, accessed November 12, 2023, https://www.lapdonline.org/lapd-motto/.

41   "Americans' Trust in Scientists, Other Groups Declines," Pew Research Center, February 15, 2022, https://www.pewresearch.org/science/2022/02/15/americans-trust-in-scientists-other-groups-declines/.

42   Ethan Winter et al., "Voters Support Protests, Have Lost Trust in Police," Data for Progress, June 6, 2020, https://www.dataforprogress.org/blog/2020/6/6/voters-support-reforms-have-lost-trust-in-police.

43   Franklin Covey, *The Nobility of Policing* (Salt Lake City, UT: Franklin Quest Publishers, 2008).

44   Melissa Russo, "NYPD Social Media Outreach Backfires When Twitter Answers #myNYPD Campaign," NBC 4 New York, April 22, 2014, https://www.nbcnewyork.com/news/local/nypd-twitter-backlash-mynypd-fail-negative-photos-flood-social-media/2001371/.

45   Eric Kowalczyk, *The Politics of Crisis* (Oceanside, CA: Indie Books International, 2008).

46 Frank Borelli, "Body Cameras: A Matter of Perspective," Officer.com, February 2022, https://www.officer.com/on-the-street/body-cameras/article/21251789/body-cameras-a-matter-of-perspective.

47 Ortal Hadad, "Podcasts: The History of Podcasts & When They Were Invented," Riverside, October 17, 2023, https://riverside.fm/blog/podcasts.

48 M. L. Ruscscak, *Make This Year Your Best Year: Podcasting Your Way to Success* (Lucas, OH: Trient Press, 2023).

49 "As Podcast Advertising Grows, Brand Lift Data Can Help Brands Demystify the ROI of Their Spending," Nielsen, September 2023, https://www.nielsen.com/insights/2023/as-podcast-advertising-grows-brand-lift-data-can-help-brands-demystify-the-roi-of-their-spending/.

50 "Making the Connection Between Podcast Fans and Their Purchase Behavior," Nielsen, https://www.nielsen.com/insights/2017/making-the-connection-between-podcast-fans-and-their-purchase-behavior/.

51 "Podcast Statistics and Data," March 7, 2023, Buzzsprout, https://www.buzzsprout.com/blog/podcast-statistics.

52 Siobhan McHugh, *The Power of Podcasting*, (New York: Columbia University Press, 2022).

53 Dan Solomon, "The Arlington Police Department Takes a Different Approach After Christian Taylor's Death," *Texas Monthly* August 12, 2015, https://www.texasmonthly.com/the-daily-post/the-arlington-police-department-has-a-very-different-approach-in-the-wake-of-christian-taylors-death/.

54 Judy Pal, "Roundtable: Police PIOs share communication strategies in the aftermath of a school shooting," Police1.com, May 20, 2023, https://www.police1.com/active-shooter/articles/roundtable-police-pios-share-communication-strategies-in-the-aftermath-of-a-school-shooting-FYTsz6sr3bi08

55 Richard Nordquist, "Sound Bites in Communication," ThoughtCo., March 11, 2020, https://www.thoughtco.com/sound-bite-communication-1691978.

56 "The Incredible Shrinking Sound Bite," *NPR News*, January 5, 2011, https://www.npr.org/2011/01/05/132671410/Congressional-Sound-Bites.

57   Antonio Oftelie, "How Relational Policing is Saving Lives with Chief Art Acevedo," Mark43, March 21, 2019, https://mark43.com/resources/podcast/episode-4-how-relational-policing-is-saving-lives-with-chief-art-acevedo/.

58   "What Cops Want in 2022," Police1, February 28, 2022, https://www.police1.com/police-products/body-cameras/articles/digital-edition-what-cops-want-in-2022-CkFK0jUZrpFOUjeR/.

59   Marcel Schwantes, "2 Sentences That Will Teach You the Best Leadership Lesson You May Hear Today," *Inc.*, March 30, 2023, https://www.inc.com/marcel-schwantes/2-sentences-that-will-teach-you-best-leadership-lesson-you-may-hear-today.html.

60   Erik Fritsvold, "Police Communication Skills Matter More Than Ever: Here's Why," University of San Diego, accessed October 21, 2023, https://onlinedegrees.sandiego.edu/police-communication-important-today/.

61   "Supporting Culture Change through Internal Communication with Officers and Civilian Staff," International Association of Chiefs of Police, accessed November 12, 2023, https://www.theiacp.org/sites/default/files/243806_IACP_CPE_Supporting_Culture_Change.pdf.

62   Amanda Hetler, "What Is ChatGPT?" TechTarget.com, October 2023, https://www.techtarget.com/whatis/definition/ChatGPT.

63   Hannah Macready, "How to Use ChatGPT for Social Media + 46 Prompts to Get Started," Hootsuite, May 31, 2023, https://blog.hootsuite.com/chatgpt-social-media/.

64   "Why People Like To Read," Pew Research Center, April 5, 2012, https://www.pewresearch.org/internet/2012/04/05/why-people-like-to-read/.